AMAZING SPORTS TRIVIA

600 QUESTIONS IN 12 CATEGORIES

MICHAEL SCHLUETER

AMAZING SPORTS TRIVIA

Michael Schlueter
Copyright 2021 Michael Schlueter

ISBN 9798453967957

Dedication

For fun loving sports trivia fans everywhere.

AMAZING SPORTS TRIVIA

Hello and welcome sports trivia fans! Start warming up those brain cells as you get set to turn these pages! Featuring 600 multiple-choice style questions in 12 popular sports categories! Winners, losers, facts and stats. Amazing, intriguing, and sometimes quirky - they're all here!

So, sit back, relax, and put your sports trivia knowledge to the test! It's sure to be a huge hit with lots of laughs at your next party with family and friends. Hey, who knows, you might even learn something!

A quick note – Records were meant to be broken. Some last for many years, even decades, while others are broken each year. So, while the stats and facts contained in this book were accurate to the best of my knowledge when it was published, inevitably, by the time this book finds its way into your hands, some of these records may be out of date. However, I'm confident this won't spoil the fun and challenge of playing the game.

Have fun and I hope you enjoy! All the Best!

Michael

CONTENTS

 FOOTBALL

1. What game was the coldest ever played in NFL history?

a) Buffalo Bills vs St. Louis Cardinals in 1975

b) Dallas Cowboys vs Green Bay Packers in 1967

c) Minnesota Vikings vs Detroit Lions in 1980

2. In what year was the first NFL game televised?

a) 1941

b) 1953

c) 1939

3. Who is the only coach to win both a Super Bowl and a Rose Bowl?

a) Dick Vermeil

b) Bill Belichick

c) Don Shula

Answers

1. (b) The coldest NFL game ever played was termed the "Ice Bowl." It pitted the Dallas Cowboys vs the Green Bay Packers at Green Bay's Lambeau Field in 1967. Temperatures reached minus 18 degrees.

2. (c) In 1939 the Brooklyn Dodgers played the Philadelphia Eagles in what would be the first televised NFL game, which was aired by NBC.

3. (a) Dick Vermeil – In 1999 with the St. Louis Rams and in 1976 at the Rose Bowl with UCLA.

4. Before the NFL mandated the use of helmets in 1943, who was the last player not to use one?

a) Chicago Bears lineman Dick Plasman
b) Philadelphia Eagles running back Steve Van Buren
c) Los Angeles Rams quarterback Bob Waterfield

5. Which NFL team is known as the "Aints" when on a losing streak?

a) Cleveland Browns
b) Seattle Seahawks
c) New Orleans Saints

6. What two teams played the first ever college football game?

a) Yale and Harvard
b) Princeton and Rutgers
c) Cornell and Dartmouth

Answers

4. (a) Before the helmet mandate by the NFL in 1943, Chicago Bears lineman Dick Plasman was the last player to not wear a helmet during a game.

5. (c) In 1980 the New Orleans Saints lost their first 14 games, prompting fans and supporters to refer to them as "Aints" instead of "Saints."

6. (b) The first college football game ever played was Princeton versus Rutgers on November 6, 1869 and was won by Rutgers 6-4.

7. What college team did football legend "Bear" Bryant coach?

a) University of Tennessee
b) University of Mississippi
c) University of Alabama

8. How many cows does it take to supply the NFL with enough leather for a year's supply of footballs?

a) 500
b) 1800
c) 3000

9. What is the oldest stadium still in use in the NFL?

a) Soldier Field in Chicago
b) Lambeau Field in Green Bay
c) Los Angeles Memorial Coliseum

Answers

7. (c) Revered coaching legend, Paul "Bear" Bryant was the head coach at the University of Alabama from 1958-1983 and amassed 6 national championships and 13 conference championships while there.

8. (c) It takes 3000 cows to supply the NFL with enough leather for a year's supply of footballs.

9. (c) The oldest stadium still in use by the NFL is the Los Angeles Memorial Coliseum. It was built in 1923.

10. What part of a football players anatomy is at greatest risk for injury?
a) Their Knee
b) Their Head
c) Their Fingers

11. In 1910, a football team was penalized how many yards for an incomplete forward pass?
a) 20 Yards
b) 5 Yards
c) 15 Yards

12. In the NFL, how many footballs are the home team required to provide for each game?
a) 16
b) 24
c) 11

Answers

10. (a) The knee is the part of a football players anatomy at greatest risk for injury.
11. (c) A 15 Yard penalty was imposed on a team in 1910 for an incomplete forward pass.
12. (b) The NFL requires the home team to provide 24 footballs for each game.

13. In what year did ABC's Monday Night Football premiere?

a) 1968

b) 1973

c) 1970

14. In what year was the first Super Bowl played?

a) 1965

b) 1967

c) 1969

15. What NFL quarterback holds the league record for most career touchdown passes?

a) Brett Favre

b) Tom Brady

c) Peyton Manning

Answers

13. (c) ABC's Monday Night Football premiered in 1970. The New York Jets took on the Cleveland Browns. Cleveland won 31-21 intercepting Joe Namath 3 times.

14. (b) The first Super Bowl was played in1967. The Green Bay Packers defeated the Kansas City Chiefs 34-10.

15. (b) Tom Brady holds this record with 581 career touchdown passes.

16. Which NFL team is the first to win three Super Bowls?
a) New England Patriots
b) Green Bay Packers
c) Pittsburgh Steelers

17. What NFL team has never played in a Super Bowl?
a) Cleveland Browns
b) San Diego Chargers
c) New Orleans Saints

18. What Motown singer tried out for the Detroit Lions in 1970?
a) Smokey Robinson
b) Stevie Wonder
c) Marvin Gaye

Answers

16. (c) The Pittsburgh Steelers. They won Super Bowls IX (in 1975), Super Bowl X (in 1976) and Super Bowl XIII (in 1979).
17. (a) Despite coming close on several occasions, the Cleveland Browns have never made it to the Super Bowl.
18. (c) In 1970, Motown singing legend Marvin Gaye tried out for the Detroit Lions.

19. Who was the first player to rush for 1000 yards in a season?
a) Beattie Feathers
b) Steve Van Buren
c) Jim Brown

20. Who was the first player drafted in the first NFL draft in 1936?
a) Bart Starr
b) Sammy Baugh
c) Jay Berwanger

21. Which player holds the NFL record for the longest interception return?
a) Ed Reed
b) Deion Sanders
c) Ronnie Lott

Answers

19. (a) Beattie Feathers, of the Chicago Bears, rushed for 1004 yards in 1934, and did it with only 119 carries.
20. (c) Jay Berwanger, originally drafted by Philadelphia, his rights were sold to the Bears, but he never signed a contract-instead taking a job as a foam-rubber salesman.
21. (a) In 2008, Ed Reed of the Baltimore Ravens set a record of 107 yards on a pass interception return. He also holds the second longest reception return (106 yards in 2004).

22. What NFL team scored the most points in a single Super Bowl?

a) Dallas Cowboys
b) Green Bay Packers
c) San Francisco 49ers

23. Which NFL Team has played in both the AFC and NFC Championship Games?

a) Seattle Seahawks
b) San Francisco 49ers
c) Jacksonville Jaguars

24. Which player supposedly put a fifty-year curse on the Detroit Lions?

a) Earl Morrall
b) Dutch Clark
c) Bobby Layne

Answers

22. (c) The San Francisco 49ers defeated the Denver Broncos in Super Bowl XXIV by a score of 55 to 10.
23. (a) Seattle Seahawks. They've won the AFC Game three times and lost the NFC Game once.
24. (c) Bobby Layne. Angered by his trade from the Lions to the Steelers in 1958, Layne predicted the Lions would "not win for fifty years."

25. Who is the only starting quarterback not to win a Super Bowl with two different teams?

a) Brett Favre

b) Tom Brady

c) Peyton Manning

26. What are the only two teams from the NFL's founding franchises that remain active?

a) Bears & Cardinals

b) Packers & Browns

c) Vikings & Giants

27. How many playoff games did the Cardinals win during their 28-year stay in St. Louis?

a) Zero

b) Six

c) Two

Answers

25. (a) Brett Favre. Peyton Manning won Super Bowls with the Indianapolis Colts and the Denver Broncos. Tom Brady won Super Bowls with the New England Patriots and the Tampa Bay Buccaneers.

26. (a) The Decatur Staleys (now the Chicago Bears) and the Chicago Cardinals (now the Arizona Cardinals) are the only two founding franchises that remain active.

27. (a) Zero. The St. Louis Cardinals advanced to the playoffs 3 times, but never won a single game.

28. Who is the only Super Bowl MVP to have played on the losing team?
a) Larry Csonka
b) Len Dawson
c) Chuck Howley

29. Which running back set an NFL record with 40 points in a single game?
a) Jim Thorpe
b) Ernie Nevers
c) Emmitt Smith

30. What team was originally named the New York Titans?
a) Tennessee Titans
b) New York Giants
c) New York Jets

Answers

28. (c) Chuck Howley. The MVP has come from the winning team every year except 1971, when Dallas Cowboys linebacker Chuck Howley won the award despite the Cowboys' loss in Super Bowl V to the Baltimore Colts.

29. (b) Ernie Nevers. On Thanksgiving Day 1929, Ernie Nevers scored all 40 points in the Cardinals' 40-6 victory over the Chicago Bears.

30. (c) New York Jets. Originally named the Titans, it changed to the Jets in 1963.

 FOOTBALL

31. Who became the head coach of the Oakland raiders in 1963?

a) John Madden

b) Al Davis

c) Art Shell

32. Who was the first African American player in Washington Redskins team history?

a) Charley Taylor

b) Art Monk

c) Bobby Mitchell

33. What was the original name of the Kansas City Chiefs?

a) Colonels

b) Wolverines

c) Texans

Answers

31. (b) Al Davis became head coach of the Oakland Raiders in 1963.

32. (c) Running back Bobby Mitchell was traded to the Redskins in 1962, becoming the first African American player for that team and became one of their greatest stars.

33. (c) Texans. The team was originally founded in 1960 as the Dallas Texans.

34. How many times did the Baltimore Ravens Ray Lewis lead the league in tackles?

a) 4

b) 5

c) 7

35. What was the nickname of the Minnesota Vikings' defensive line from the late 1960s to the late 1970s?

a) Fearsome Four

b) Purple Crush

c) Purple People Eaters

36. Which team did the Miami Dolphins beat to claim their first Super Bowl victory?

a) Minnesota Vikings

b) San Francisco 49ers

c) Washington Redskins

Answers

34. (b) Ray Lewis led the NFL in tackles five times. (1997, 1999, 2001, 2003 and 2004).

35. (c) Purple People Eaters. This was in reference to a popular song from 1958, the efficiency of the defense, and the color of their uniforms.

36. (c) In Super Bowl VII, the Dolphins defeated the Washington Redskins 14-7.

37. What was the name of the no-huddle offense the Buffalo Bills used under head coach Marv Levy?

a) K-Gun

b) West Coast

c) Air Coryell

38. Who is often referred to as the "Father of American Football?"

a) Jonathan Sanders

b) Walter Camp

c) Frederic Long

39. What company made the first Vince Lombardi Trophy awarded each year to the winners of the NFL Super Bowl?

a) Tiffany & Company

b) Jostens

c) Wilson Trophy

Answers

37. (a) K-Gun. Employing the "K-Gun" offense, known for its no-huddle shotgun formations, QB Jim Kelly led the Bills to a record four consecutive Super Bowls.

38. (b) Walter Camp, a Yale medical student and team captain, is credited with developing rules and a set of "downs" helping evolve the game to its current form.

39. (a) Tiffany & Company. First awarded to the Green Bay Packers on January 15, 1967.

40. What Cincinnati Bengals player legally changed his name to match his jersey number?

a) A.J. Green
b) Ickey Woods
c) Chad Johnson

41. Who is the New York Jets all-time leading scorer?

a) Curtis Martin
b) Pat Leahy
c) Emerson Boozer

42. What player holds the record for the most fumbles in a Super Bowl?

a) Terry Bradshaw
b) Roger Staubach
c) Jim Kelly

Answers

40. (c) Chad Johnson. On August 29, 2008, Johnson legally changed his name to Ochocinco ("Eight Five") in Spanish to match his jersey number. In 2012, he legally changed his name back to Johnson.
41. (b) Pat Leahy. Placekicker Leahy played 18 seasons with the Jets, accumulating a franchise record of 1470 points.
42. (b) Roger Staubach of the Dallas Cowboys. He fumbled the ball five times in four Super Bowl appearances.

43. Who was the headliner of the first Super Bowl Halftime show?
a) Elvis Presley
b) The Three Stooges
c) Ella Fitzgerald

44. What interrupted play in Super Bowl XLVII for 34 minutes?
a) Injured player
b) Power outage
c) Rain

45. What was unusual about the coin flipped for Super Bowl XLIV?
a) It contained a hologram
b) It was shaped like John Madden's head
c) It was from outer space

Answers

43. (b) The Three Stooges. Also performing was trumpeter Al Hurt, two college marching bands, two men in jet packs, and 300 pigeons.
44. (b) A power outage. Baltimore had built a 28-6 lead when in the third quarter a power outage in the Superdome suspended play for 34 minutes, earning the game the nickname, the "Blackout Bowl".
45. (c) It was from outer space. The coin toss featured a coin that had spent the previous 11 days orbiting the Earth on a NASA space mission.

46. What quarterback led the Tampa Bay Buccaneers to their first winning season?

a) Steve Spurrier
b) Vinnie Testaverde
c) Doug Williams

47. What year did the AFL and NFL officially merge into one league?

a) 1970
b) 1967
c) 1981

48. What NFL star is the only person to play in both a Super Bowl and a World Series game?

a) Deion Sanders
b) Steve Young
c) Joe Montana

Answers

46. (c) Doug Williams. After winning just two games in the first two years of the franchise, Williams led the Buccaneers to the playoffs three times in five seasons.

47. (a) 1970. The AFL was formed in 1960 to create competition with the NFL (created in 1920). The merging in 1970 created the championship game known as the Super Bowl.

48. (a) Deion Sanders was in Super Bowl XXIX and XXX. He was also in the 1992 World Series.

49. What NFL team is the only publicly owned franchise in the league?

a) Green Bay Packers

b) New York Giants

c) Kansas City Chiefs

50. How many sets of fathers and sons have played in the NFL?

a) 23

b) 224

c) 486

Answers

49. (a) Green Bay Packers. The Packers have been a publicly owned, non-profit corporation since August 18, 1923. All other NFL teams are privately owned.

50. (b) 224 sets of fathers and sons have played in the NFL. There have also been 348 sets of brothers who have played in the NFL.

Alright sports fans! I hope you enjoyed those fun and tantalizing bits of football trivia! Were you as smart as you thought you were?

Now, get ready! We're trading the gridiron for the diamond next! On to another great American sport…BASEBALL!

 BASEBALL

1. **What pitcher holds the record for most complete games in an MLB career?**
a) Cy Young
b) Nolan Ryan
c) Don Sutton

2. **What major league player retired with the same number of home runs as his father?**
a) Prince Fielder
b) Cal Ripken Jr
c) Roberto Alomar

3. **What player has the most hits in MLB history?**
a) Derek Jeter
b) Ty Cobb
c) Pete Rose

Answers

1. (a) Cy Young. He pitched 749 complete games over the course of his 22- year career. Only two other pitchers have even started that many games, Nolan Ryan and Don Sutton.
2. (a) Prince Fielder ended his career with 319 home runs, the same number as his father, Cecil Fielder.
3. (c) Pete Rose of the Cincinnati Reds, a switch hitter, is the all-time MLB leader in hits (4,256), games played (3,562), at-bats (14,053), singles (3,215), and outs (10,328).

4. Against what opposing team did Babe Ruth hit his first career home run?
a) Chicago Cubs
b) New York Yankees
c) Boston Red Sox

5. What year was the first World Series played?
a) 1910
b) 1921
c) 1903

6. What player holds the record for the most World Series home runs?
a) Lou Gehrig
b) Mickey Mantle
c) Hank Aaron

Answers

4. (b) New York Yankees. While playing for the Red Sox, Ruth hit his first career home run against the Yankees on May 6, 1915.
5. (c) 1903. The Boston Americans beat the Pittsburgh Pirates, winning five games in a best-of-nine series.
6. (b) Mickey Mantle of the New York Yankees. He played in 12 World Series hitting 18 home runs. He also holds the records for most runs (42), runs batted in (40), and total bases (123).

7. Who was the first father and son to play MLB as teammates?

a) Cal Ripken & Cal Ripken Jr.

b) Ken Griffey & Ken Griffey Jr.

c) Cecil Fielder & Prince Fielder

8. Who was the first woman to regularly host Major League Baseball games for a major network?

a) Gayle Gardner

b) Erin Andrews

c) Samantha Ponder

9. Who was the first MLB player to make $1 million in a single year?

a) Catfish Hunter

b) Joe Dimaggio

c) Nolan Ryan

Answers

7. (b) Ken Griffey & Ken Griffey Jr. both played for the Seattle Mariners in 1990. On September 14, 1990 they hit back-to-back home runs, creating another father-son baseball first.

8. (a) In 1989, NBC's Gayle Gardner became the first woman to host MLB games for a major television network.

9. (c) Nolan Ryan. In 1980 he signed a four-year free agent contract with the Houston Astros for $1 million per season.

10. What Chicago Cubs pitcher also played basketball for the Harlem Globetrotters?

a) Hippo Vaughn
b) Ferguson Jenkins
c) Mordecai Brown

11. What batter claimed the Triple Crown in MLB in 2012?

a) Miguel Cabrera
b) Nolan Arenado
c) Chris Davis

12. What pitcher set a major league record in 1988 by pitching 59 consecutive innings without allowing a run?

a) Frank Viola
b) Bret Saberhagen
c) Orel Hershiser

Answers

10. (b) Ferguson Jenkins pitched for various MLB teams from 1965 thru 1983. He also played basketball for the Globetrotters from 1967 to 1969.
11. (a) Miguel Cabrera claimed the 17th MLB Triple Crown in 2012, leading the league in batting average, home runs, and RBIs. He was the first player to do so in 45 seasons.
12. (c) Orel Hershiser. He helped lead the Dodgers to a World Series victory that same year.

13. What is the most expensive baseball card?
a) Babe Ruth
b) Honus Wagner
c) Mickey Mantle

14. What was unique about St. Louis Browns outfielder Pete Gray?
a) He was legally blind
b) He played without a glove
c) He only had one arm

15. What player is credited with inventing the curveball?
a) Ted Williams
b) Sparky Lyle
c) William Cummings

Answers

13. (b) Honus Wagner. His card from the 1909-1911 American Tobacco Company set is valued at approximately 2.8 million dollars. There were only 200 ever made because Wagner didn't want to support tobacco use for his young fans.

14. (c) Despite losing his left arm in a car accident, Gray played centerfield in 77 games for the Browns in 1945.

15. (c) William Arthur "Candy" Cummings is credited with inventing this hard-to-hit pitch in the early 1870s. Its use in early years was illegal.

16. What team won the 2016 World Series?
a) Chicago Cubs
b) New York Mets
c) Kansas City Royals

17. Who is the only person to have played in the Little League World Series, the National Championship of the College World Series, the MLB World Series, Olympic Baseball, and the World Baseball Classic?
a) Jason Varitek
b) Gaylord Perry
c) Alex Rodriguez

18. What MLB player is known as Mr. Tiger?
a) Al Kaline
b) Hank Greenberg
c) Ty Cobb

Answers

16. (a) The Chicago Cubs. They defeated the Cleveland Indians, winning their first World Series in 108 years.
17. (a) Jason Varitek is the only person to have played in all five of these events.
18. (a) Al Kaline played his entire 22-year baseball career with the Detroit Tigers, mainly as a right fielder where he won ten Gold Gloves.

19. Which of the following St. Louis Cardinals hit four home runs in one game?
a) Mark Whiten
b) Stan Musial
c) Keith Hernandez

20. Who was the first player to reach 50 doubles and 50 home runs in the same season?
a) Albert Belle
b) Alex Rodriguez
c) Mark McGuire

21. Why was Babe Ruth's jersey number 3?
a) He had three brothers
b) He batted third
c) For the Holy Trinity

Answers

19. (a) Mark Whiten. On September 7, 1993, Whiten hit a grand slam, two three-run homers, and a two-run shot against the Cincinnati Reds.
20. (a) Albert Belle. In 1995, Cleveland Indians Albert Belle had 52 doubles and 50 home runs.
21. (b) Originally, jersey numbers were based on batting order, and the Babe always hit third.

22. Who was the first U.S. President to throw the ceremonial first pitch on opening day?
a) Calvin Coolidge
b) Grover Cleveland
c) William Howard Taft

23. What St. Louis Cardinal first baseman was known as "Cha-Cha"?
a) Bill White
b) Orlando Cepeda
c) Keith Hernandez

24. Who was the first Puerto Rican player to receive a World Series MVP Award?
a) Carlos Beltran
b) Roberto Clemente
c) Ivan Rodriguez

Answers

22. (c) On April 14, 1910, William Howard Taft, a former semipro baseball player, became the first U.S. President to throw the ceremonial first pitch.
23. (b) Orlando Cepeda. Also known as the "Baby Bull," Cepeda only played for the Cardinals three seasons but attained legendary status in the 1967 and 1968 seasons when the Cards went to the World Series.
24. (b) Roberto Clemente became the first Puerto Rican player to win the World Series MVP Award. (1971). He was also the first Puerto Rican player to be inducted into the Hall of Fame.

25. Who is credited with designing the modern-day baseball field?
a) William Ungersoll
b) John Francis
c) Alexander Cartright

26. How many stitches are on a baseball?
a) 108
b) 169
c) 66

27. What MLB team has the most players in the Hall of Fame?
a) Detroit Tigers
b) New York Yankees
c) Boston Red Sox

Answers

25. (c) Alexander Cartwright of New York invented the modern baseball field in 1845. He and the members of his New York Knickerbocker Baseball Club designed the rules and regulations that were accepted for the modern game of baseball.
26. (a) There are 108 double stitches on a baseball. The first and last stitches are completely hidden. 88 inches of waxed red thread are used per baseball.
27. (b) The New York Yankees. They have 26 inductees in the Hall of Fame.

28. Who was the first Texas Ranger to throw a perfect game?
a) Nolan Ryan
b) Charlie Hough
c) Kenny Rogers

29. Which Boston Red Sox player was known as the "Splendid Splinter?"
a) Ted Williams
b) Carl Yastrzemski
c) Jim Rice

30. How many All-Star Game appearances did Willie Mays of the San Francisco Giants make?
a) 20
b) 14
c) 9

Answers

28. (c) On July 28, 1994, Kenny Rogers pitched the 14th perfect game in Major League Baseball history, defeating the California Angels 4-0 at The Ballpark at Arlington.
29. (a) Ted Williams, known as the "Splendid Splinter," hit 521 home runs during his career with the Red Sox.
30. (a) Willie Mays had 20 consecutive All Star game appearances from 1954-1973.

 BASEBALL

31. St. Louis Cardinal superstar Stan Musial was widely known for playing what musical instrument?

a) banjo

b) piano

c) harmonica

32. Which player did NOT hit at least 10 World Series home runs during his career?

a) Mickey Mantle

b) Babe Ruth

c) Joe Dimaggio

33. One player in Brave history played for the Boston, Milwaukee, and Atlanta Braves. Who was he?

a) Hank Aaron

b) Babe Ruth

c) Eddie Mathews

Answers

31. (c) Harmonica. Musial regularly performed "Take Me Out to the Ballpark" at the Hall of Fame induction ceremony and was even on the television show "Hee Haw."

32. (c) Joe Dimaggio. He only hit 8. Ruth hit 15 and Mantle retired with a record 18 World Series home runs.

33. (c) Eddie Mathews spent 1 year with the franchise in Boston, 13 years in Milwaukee, and 1 year in Atlanta.

34. What trophy is presented to the winners of the World Series?
a) Warren G. Giles Trophy
b) Lombardi Trophy
c) Commissioner's Trophy

35. Who did the Anaheim Angels beat to win their first World Series in 2002?
a) San Francisco Giants
b) St. Louis Cardinals
c) Cincinnati Reds

36. What former Chicago Cub player is known as "Mr. Cub"?
a) Hank Sauer
b) Ernie Banks
c) Fergie Jenkins

Answers

34. (c) The Commissioner's Trophy is presented each year by the Commissioner of Baseball to the Major League Baseball team that wins the World Series.
35. (a) The San Francisco Giants. The Angels defeated the Giants in seven games and after waiting 61 years, finally won their first World Series.
36. (b) Ernie Banks. One of the Cubs' most popular players, Banks hit more home runs (248) than anyone in the majors during 1955 to 1960, including Mickey Mantle, Henry Aaron, and Willie Mays.

37. What Los Angeles Dodger pitcher broke a 62-year record when he struck out 29 batters in the 1965 World Series?

a) Sandy Koufax

b) Don Drysdale

c) Mudcat Grant

38. What did Pittsburgh Pirates pitcher Dock Ellis claim to have done on June 12, 1970?

a) Pitch a no-hitter on LSD

b) Bribed an umpire

c) Talk to the ghost of Babe Ruth

39. What team was accused of intentionally losing the 1919 World Series in exchange for money from a gambling syndicate led by Arthur Rothstein?

a) Boston Red Sox

b) Chicago White Sox

c) Detroit Tigers

Answers

37. (a) Sandy Koufax. He finished the World Series with a 0.38 ERA, 29 strikeouts, and World Series MVP honors.
38. (a) Pitch a no-hitter on LSD. Remembering only bits and pieces of the game, at one point he thought Richard Nixon was the home plate umpire, and Jimi Hendrix the batter.
39. (b) The Chicago White Sox, afterward often referred to as the Chicago "Black Sox."

40. In what year was there no World Series played?
a) 1923
b) 1945
c) 1994

41. Who was the first baseball player to appear on a Wheaties cereal box?
a) Lou Gehrig
b) Joe Dimaggio
c) Babe Ruth

42. What famous criminal was once a semi-professional baseball player?
a) Lucky Luciano
b) Al Capone
c) John Dillinger

Answers

40. (c) 1994. On August 24, 1994, MLB went on strike due to the lack of consensus on a collective bargaining agreement between the Players Association and MLB. It was the longest (232 days) in history and cancelled the rest of the season, and for the first time since 1904, the World Series.

41. (a) Lou Gehrig. In 1934, Lou won the Triple Crown batting title and became the first baseball player to appear on a Wheaties cereal box. (He appeared on the back, not the front.)

42. (c) John Dillinger. During 1924 Dillinger played shortstop for the Martinsville Athletics.

43. What player hit the "Shot Heard Round the World"?
a) Bobby Thompson
b) Ralph Kiner
c) Gus Zernial

44. How many baseballs are used during a typical Major League game?
a) 30
b) 50
c) 100

45. Who is the first player since Babe Ruth to pitch 50 innings and hit 15 home runs in a single season?
a) Don Newcombe
b) Micah Owings
c) Shohei Ohtani

Answers

43. (a) Bobby Thompson. On October 3, 1951, New York Giants outfielder Bobby Thompson homered off Brooklyn Dodgers pitcher Ralph Branca to win the game and clinch the National League pennant.
44. (c) 100. This equates to just a few pitches per ball. Once the balls are removed from the game they're recycled for batting practice.
45. (c) Shohei Ohtani. On September 2, 2018, Angels pitcher and designated hitter Shohei Ohtani, tied Ruth's record and accomplished something that hadn't been done since 1919.

46. How many baseballs could Cincinnati Reds catcher Johnny Bench, hold in one hand?

a) 5

b) 6

c) 7

47. What MLB player holds the record for most stolen bases in a single season?

a) Vince Coleman

b) Lou Brock

c) Rickey Henderson

48. Which player has had the longest career in Major League Baseball?

a) Pete Rose

b) Nolan Ryan

c) Tommy John

Answers

46. (c) 7. Johnny Bench could hold 7 baseballs in his right hand at one time.

47. (c) Rickey Henderson holds the record, stealing 130 bases in the 1982 season. He's followed by Lou Brock who had 118 in 1974 and coming in third is Vince Coleman who stole 110 in 1985.

48. (b) Nolan Ryan holds the record with a Major League career of 27 years, pitching for four different teams, the Mets, Angels, Astros, and Rangers.

49. Who was the shortest man to ever play Major League Baseball?

a) Freddie Patek

b) Rabbit Maranville

c) Eddie Gaedel

50. What "secret ingredient" is rubbed on every new baseball before they're used in a game?

a) Mud

b) Tobacco juice

c) Pine tar

Answers

49. (c) Eddie Gaedel. On August 19, 1951, the St. Louis Browns sent Eddie Gaedel (3feet, 7 inches) to the batter's box in a publicity stunt. He took a four-pitch walk and trotted down to first base. Brown's owner Bill Veeck said, "He was, by golly, the best darn midget to ever play big-league ball. He was also the only one."

50. (a) For 80 years, Major League Baseball has rubbed Lena Blackburne 'Baseball Rubbing Mud' into their new balls to break them in and take the gloss off. The mud is a very fine, unique mud that comes from a secret location near Palmyra, New Jersey.

Well, did you hit it out of the park? Or strike out? Either way, I hope you had a few, "Wow, never knew that one" moments!

Alright, time to swap out the bats and gloves and head to the hardwood. That's right - it's time for some BASKETBALL!

1. Who was the only person in NBA history to be named Most Valuable Player, Coach of the Year, and Executive of the Year?

a) Earvin "Magic" Johnson Jr.

b) Larry Bird

c) Bill Russell

2. Who was drafted in the 7th round of the 1977 NBA draft?

a) Larry Bird

b) Bruce Jenner

c) Terry Bradshaw

3. Why did Michael Jordon wear No. 12 instead of his traditional No. 23 in an NBA game against the Orlando Magic?

a) His jersey was stolen

b) It was his 12th wedding anniversary

c) In honor of Joe Namath

Answers

1. (b) Larry Bird. He won 3 NBA Championships, 2 NBA Finals MVP Awards with the Celtics. He then served as head coach and ultimately as president of basketball operations for the Indiana Pacers.

2. (b) Bruce Jenner. Jenner was drafted No. 139 by the Kansas City Kings after winning the men's decathlon at the 1976 Olympics.

3. (a) Jordon's jersey was stolen the day of the game. They had no backup jersey for Jordon but used an extra No. 12 that didn't have a name on it.

4. Which of the following players was drafted ahead of Michael Jordon in the 1984 NBA draft?
a) Kareem Abdul-Jabbar
b) Charles Barkley
c) Hakeem Olajuwon

5. Who is the only coach to win both an NCAA and a NBA Championship?
a) Jerry Tarkanian
b) Chuck Daily
c) Larry Brown

6. Who holds the record for most rebounds in a single NBA game?
a) Wilt Chamberlain
b) Larry Bird
c) Michael Jordon

Answers

4. (c) Hakeem Olajuwon was drafted first overall by the Houston Rockets. He led them to Championships in 1994 and 1995, and was inducted into the Hall of Fame in 2008.

5. (c) Larry Brown won the 1988 NCAA Division 1 Title at the University of Kansas. He made coaching history by leading the Detroit Pistons to an NBA Championship in 2004.

6. (a) Wilt Chamberlain. On November 24, 1960 Philadelphia Warrior Wilt Chamberlain set an NBA record with 55 rebounds in a game against the Boston Celtics.

7. What team holds the record for the most consecutive NBA titles?
a) Los Angeles Lakers
b) Chicago Bulls
c) Boston Celtics

8. What is the diameter of a regulation basketball hoop?
a) 18 inches
b) 15 inches
c) 12 inches

9. What new kind of shot did Joe Fulks score a record 63 points with, in one game in 1949?
a) Jump shot
b) Hook shot
c) Three-point shot

Answers

7. (c) The Boston Celtics hold the NBA record of winning 8 consecutive Championships from 1959-1966.
8. (a) Eighteen inches.
9. (a) Jump shot. On February 10, 1949, "Jumping Joe" Fulks introduced the 'jump shot', scoring a then-NBA record of 63 points against the Indianapolis Jets.

10. What player was known as the "Clown Prince" of the Harlem Globetrotters?
a) Fred "Curly" Neal
b) Goose Tatum
c) Meadowlark Lemon

11. Who is considered the creator of the game of basketball as we know it today?
a) James Naismith
b) Walter Wingfield
c) William G. Morgan

12. In what year was the first NBA basketball game played?
a) 1933
b) 1946
c) 1952

Answers

10. (c) Meadowlark Lemon. For 22 years he was known as the "Clown Prince" of the Harlem Globetrotters. He played in more than 16,000 games for the Globetrotters.
11. (a) Dr. James Naismith is credited with inventing the game of basketball in December, 1891, in Springfield, Massachusetts. Initially, peach baskets and a soccer style ball were used.
12. (b) The first game in NBA (then known as the BAA) history was played on November 1, 1946 in Toronto, Canada between the New York Knicks and the Toronto Huskies.

13. What NBA player retired unexpectedly on November 7, 1991?

a) Michael Jordon
b) Kobe Bryant
c) Earvin "Magic" Johnson

14. What NBA teammates were nicknamed the "Splash Brothers"?

a) Michael Jordon & Scottie Pippen
b) Jerry West & Wilt Chamberlain
c) Stephen Curry & Klay Thompson

15. Who was the shortest player in NBA history?

a) Spud Webb
b) Earl Boykins
c) Muggsy Bogues

Answers

13. (c) Earvin "Magic" Johnson retired on November 7, 1991, after disclosing that he had tested positive for the HIV virus. He helped lead the Lakers to five NBA titles.

14. (c) Golden State Warriors Stephen Curry and Klay Thompson became known as the "Splash Brothers". During the 2013-14 season they set an NBA record for combined three-pointers in a season with 484.

15. (c) Point guard Muggsy Bogues was the shortest player in NBA history at 5 ft 3 in.

16. What NBA player was nicknamed "Houdini of the Hardwood"?
a) Oscar Robertson
b) Bob Cousy
c) Bill Russell

17. Who was the only Harlem Globetrotters player to win League MVP in the NBA?
a) Wilt Chamberlain
b) Moses Malone
c) Meadowlark Lemon

18. St. Louis was home to two NBA teams. Who were they?
a) Arches and Brewers
b) Bombers and Hawks
c) Cyclones and Eagles

Answers

16. (b) Bob Cousy. Known as "Houdini of the Hardwood", Cousy had a very successful career with the Boston Celtics winning the NBA MVP Award in 1957, appearing in 13 NBA All-Star Games and playing in six Championship games.

17. (a) Wilt "The Stilt" Chamberlain played for the Harlem Globetrotters (1958-59) before joining the NBA where he would earn 4 League MVP Awards.

18. (b) The St. Louis Bombers (1949-50) and the St. Louis Hawks (1955-68). The Hawks won the NBA Title in 1958.

19. What team has won the most NCAA Basketball Championships?
a) UCLA
b) University of Kentucky
c) University of North Carolina

20. What company has made the official NBA game basketball since 1983?
a) Wilson
b) Spaulding
c) Rawlings

21. From 1967 to 1976, the American Basketball Association used a ball with three distinctive colors on it. Which colors were they?
a) Black, Red, and White
b) Gold, White, and Blue
c) Red, White, and Blue

Answers

19. (a) UCLA holds this record with 11 Men's Championships, 10 of these being coached by John Wooden.

20. (b) Spaulding was the first company to produce the first dedicated basketball in the last years of the 19th century and has produced the NBA's official game ball since 1983.

21. (c) Red, White, and Blue. Created by George Mikan, the first ABA Commissioner, the ball reflected the "cool and hip" style of the new league, along with a patriotic look as well.

22. What NBA player scored 100 points on March 2, 1962?

a) Elgin Baylor
b) Wilt Chamberlain
c) Bill Russell

23. Who scored the first three-point basket in NBA history?

a) Larry Bird
b) Bill Russell
c) Chris Ford

24. What player never fouled out of a regular-season or playoff game in his 14 years in the NBA?

a) Larry Bird
b) Wilt Chamberlain
c) Michael Jordon

Answers

22. (b) Wilt Chamberlain. On March 2, 1962, Chamberlain of the Philadelphia Warriors, scored 100 points, the most ever by an NBA player in a single game, during his team's 169-147 win over the New York Knicks.

23. (c) On October 12, 1979, Chris Ford of the Boston Celtics scored the first three-point basket in NBA history against the Houston Rockets.

24. (b) Wilt Chamberlain holds this record. He never fouled out once in his 14 season, 1,205 game career.

25. What team holds the record for the longest winning streak in NBA history?
a) Los Angeles Lakers
b) Chicago Bulls
c) Golden State Warriors

26. Who is the NBA Championship Trophy named after?
a) James Naismith
b) Larry O'Brien
c) Red Auerbach

27. What NBA player was thrown out of a record 127 games?
a) Kareem Abdul-Jabbar
b) Vern Mikkelsen
c) Dennis Rodman

Answers

25. (a) The Los Angeles Lakers won 33 straight games in the 1971-72 season, an NBA record.
26. (b) Larry O'Brien. Originally called the Walter A. Brown Trophy for the former Celtics owner whose name had been on the league's previous championship trophy, it was renamed in 1984, to honor outgoing NBA commissioner Larry O'Brien.
27. (b) Vern Mikkelsen was a power forward for the Minneapolis Lakers from 1949-1959 and holds the NBA record for being thrown out of 127 games during his career.

28. What player is credited with performing the first "slam dunk"?
a) Bob Kurland
b) Bill Russell
c) Nathaniel Clifton

29. What are the dimensions of a regulation size NBA basketball court?
a) 94 feet by 50 feet
b) 100 feet by 60 feet
c) 75 feet by 45 feet

30. At what distance was the longest shot ever made in an NBA game?
a) 58 feet
b) 89 feet
c) 107 feet

Answers

28. (a) Bob Kurland. Kurland, who was a star player for Oklahoma State is credited with making the first "slam dunk" in a game against Temple University in 1944. In the 1940s, dunks weren't a big part of basketball and weren't celebrated like they are in today's game.
29. (a) 94 feet by 50 feet is the size of a regulation NBA basketball court.
30. (b) 89 feet. On February 17, 2001, Baron Davis of the Charlotte Hornets sunk an 89 foot shot with 0.7 seconds remaining in the third quarter against the Milwaukee Bucks.

31. What is the penalty for having more than five players from a team on the court during live play?
a) Technical foul
b) Personal foul
c) Forfeiture of one timeout

32. What player holds the NBA record for most career points?
a) Michael Jordon
b) Kareem Abdul-Jabbar
c) Karl Malone

33. What year did the NBA introduce the 24-second shot clock?
a) 1946
b) 1954
c) 1974

Answers

31. (a) Technical foul. The offended team is awarded one free throw.
32. (b) Kareem Abdul-Jabbar. He holds this NBA record with a total of 38,387 total career points.
33. (b) 1954. The NBA introduced the 24-second shot clock during the 1954-55 season to speed up the game. Syracuse Nationals owner Danny Biasone devised the number 24 by dividing the game's 48 minutes into 120, the average of 60 shots per team in games played from the previous three seasons.

34. What brawl in 2004 involving both players and fans became known as the worst in NBA history?

a) 'Malice in the Palace'

b) 'Mayhem in Miami'

c) 'Brutality in Boston'

35. What horrifying injury occurred to Villanova player Allen Ray during a 2006 college basketball tournament game?

a) His eye popped out

b) He broke his leg in 4 places

c) Two fingers were severed off

36. Which of the following basketballs will bounce higher?

a) a warm basketball

b) a cold basketball

c) they will bounce the same

Answers

34. (a) 'Malice in the Palace' became known as the worst brawl in NBA history when on November 19, 2004, during an Indiana Pacers and Detroit Pistons game, 9 NBA players were suspended and 5 fans received criminal charges.

35. (a) Ray's eye popped out after a Pittsburgh player injured it. Doctors were able to pop the eye back in, and he regained his vision.

36. (a) A warm basketball will bounce higher than a cold one because the molecules in a warm ball hit its inside surface at a faster speed.

 BASKETBALL

37. Which team set an NBA record by losing 26 games in a row?
a) Cleveland Cavaliers
b) Miami Heat
c) Utah Jazz

38. Which clothing company manufactures all of the NBA uniforms?
a) Adidas
b) Nike
c) Under Armour

39. Who was the youngest player to start an NBA game?
a) Kobe Bryant
b) Jerry West
c) Michael Jordon

Answers

37. (a) The Cleveland Cavaliers lost 26 games in a row during the 2010-2011 season.
38. (b) Nike was awarded this contract in 2015 after Adidas had it for over 10 years.
39. (a) Kobe Bryant entered the NBA straight out of high school. In 1996, he was the youngest player in NBA history at that time, at 18 years, 2 months, and 11 days. He played his entire 20-year professional career for the Los Angeles Lakers.

40. How many 3-point shots did Kareem Abdul-Jabbar, one of the NBA's highest scorers, make in his 20-year career?

a) 1
b) 37
c) 84

41. In 1967, why did the NCAA ban slam dunking?

a) To make the game more fair
b) Safety concerns over shattered backboards
c) To eliminate 'showing-off' during a game

42. Why is the NBA team in Philadelphia named the "76ers"?

a) Because they joined the NBA in 1976
b) The Declaration of Independence was signed there in 1776
c) Their coach's lucky number was '76'

Answers

40. (a) 1. Kareem Abdul-Jabbar holds the NBA's record for most points in a career with 38,387, but only made one successful 3-point shot during that time.
41. (b) Citing safety concerns over shattered backboard glass, the NCAA banned slam-dunking in 1967 for 10 years. Technology and breakaway rims eventually solved this problem.
42. (b) The "76ers" are so named because the Declaration of Independence was signed in Philadelphia in 1776.

 BASKETBALL

43. Which team is the oldest franchise in the NBA?

a) Detroit Pistons

b) Sacramento Kings

c) Boston Celtics

44. What player is silhouetted on the NBA logo?

a) Wilt Chamberlain

b) Jerry West

c) Michael Jordan

45. In an NBA game, how many minutes does each quarter last?

a) 12 minutes

b) 15 minutes

c) 20 minutes

Answers

43. (b) The Sacramento Kings are the oldest franchise in the NBA. They were founded in 1923.

44. (b) The player silhouetted in the NBA logo is former all-star Jerry West who played with the Los Angeles Lakers from 1960-1974.

45. (a) Each quarter in an NBA game lasts for 12 minutes.

46. What is the most common injury in basketball?
a) Broken Finger
b) Sprained Ankle
c) Torn Rotator Cuff

47. What type of wood are all NBA courts made of?
a) Maple
b) Pine
c) Oak

48. What was the final score of the longest game in NBA history?
a) 115 to 112
b) 135 to 133
c) 186 to 184

Answers

46. (b) A sprained ankle is the most common injury in basketball. However, knee inflammation is the injury that causes players to miss the most games.
47. (a) Maple is the wood used on all NBA basketball courts, which is strong but flexible.
48. (c) 186 to 184. On December 13, 1983, the Detroit Pistons defeated the Denver Nuggets 186 to 184 in triple overtime.

49. What player has played more games than any other player in NBA history?
a) Robert Parish
b) Bob Cousy
c) Larry Bird

50. The NBA requires all game balls to be inflated to what air pressure?
a) Between 5.5 and 6.8 PSI
b) Between 7.3 and 8.5 PSI
c) Between 9.0 and 9.5 PSI

Answers

49. (a) All-Star center Robert Parish holds the NBA record for most games played, 1,611, during his 21-year career (1976-1997). He played for the Golden State Warriors, Boston Celtics, Charlotte Hornets and the Chicago Bulls.
50. (b) All NBA game balls are required to be inflated to between 7.3 and 8.5 PSI.

I hope you slam dunked a few of those basketball trivia facts! If not, no worries. Maybe ICE HOCKEY is your strong suit!

Get set – we're headed to center ice next!!

 ICE HOCKEY

1. Who was the first NHL star to be named "Sportsman of the Year" by Sports Illustrated Magazine?
a) Bobby Orr
b) Wayne Gretzky
c) Bobby Hull

2. What NHL team has won the most Stanley Cup Championships?
a) Montreal Canadiens
b) Chicago Black Hawks
c) Pittsburgh Penguins

3. What NHL team won their first Stanley Cup in 2019 after a long 51-year wait?
a) St. Louis Blues
b) Toronto Maple Leafs
c) Detroit Rd Wings

Answers

1. (a) In 1970, Bobby Orr was the first NHL player to be named "Sportsman of the Year" by Sports Illustrated Magazine. He also won league MVP honors that year and led the Bruins to a Stanley Cup Championship.
2. (a) The Montreal Canadiens hold the NHL record for most Stanley Cup Championships with 23.
3. (a) The St. Louis Blues have qualified for the playoffs in all but nine of their 52 seasons, appeared in the Stanley Cup Finals four times, and finally won the Stanley Cup in 2019.

4. What year did the Stanley Cup have no winner?
a) 1919
b) 1944
c) 1968

5. What NHL star was referred to as the "Golden Jet"?
a) Gordie Howe
b) Bobby Hull
c) Jean Beliveau

6. What year was the offsides rule introduced by the NHL?
a) 1930
b) 1950
c) 1970

Answers

4. (a) In 1919 there was no Stanley Cup winner. The final between Montreal and Seattle was cancelled due to an influenza epidemic.

5. (b) Bobby Hull, the "Golden Jet" of the Chicago Blackhawks, won several goal-scoring titles, three overall scoring championships, and two MVP awards in the NHL in the 1960s.

6. (a) On September 27, 1930, at the annual NHL Governor's meeting, the new offsides rule was passed, stating that: "The puck must be propelled into the attacking zone before any player from the attacking team can enter that zone."

7. What player set an NHL record in 1976, with 10 points in one game?
a) Darryl Sittler
b) Phil Esposito
c) Wayne Gretzky

8. On November 1, 1959, Montreal Canadiens goalie Jacques Plante made history by doing what?
a) Becoming the first goalie in NHL history to wear a facemask.
b) Playing a record 47 games without allowing a goal.
c) Becoming the first goalie in NHL history to score a goal.

9. Legendary NHL coach Scotty Bowman won a record nine Stanley Cups during his coaching career, which lasted from 1967-2001. With which team did Bowman begin his coaching career?
a) Detroit Red Wings
b) Chicago Black Hawks
c) St. Louis Blues

Answers

7. (a) On February 7, 1976, Darryl Sittler of the Toronto Maple Leafs scored six goals and had four assists to help defeat the Boston Bruins 11-4.
8. (a) After being hit in the face by a slapshot earlier in the game, breaking his jaw, Plante made NHL history by wearing a mask for the rest of the game and career.
9. (c) Bowman started with the St. Louis Blues.

10. Which famous goaltender played in a record 502 consecutive complete NHL games?
a) Glenn Hall
b) Patrick Roy
c) Jacques Plante

11. Which NHL team was the first American team ever to enter the NHL?
a) Boston Bruins
b) New York Rangers
c) Detroit Red Wings

12. What are the dimensions (in feet) of an official NHL playing surface?
a) 175 feet by 55 feet
b) 200 feet by 85 feet
c) 219 feet by 99 feet

Answers

10. (a) Glenn Hall holds this record. This incredible streak lasted from 1955 to 1962 when he played for Detroit and Chicago.
11. (a) The Boston Bruins were the first American team to enter the NHL in 1924 as part of the league's expansion.
12. (b) 200 feet by 85 feet are the official dimensions of a regulation NHL playing surface.

13. In the 1981-82 season, Wayne Gretzky set an NHL record for the fewest number of games to score 50 goals. How many games did it take?

a) 50

b) 64

c) 39

14. The Conn Smythe Trophy is awarded to an NHL player for what?

a) Most goals scored in a single season

b) Most Valuable Player of the Stanley Cup playoffs

c) Most penalty minutes in a single season

15. Which NHL team was notoriously nicknamed the "Broad Street Bullies"?

a) Boston Bruins

b) Philadelphia Flyers

c) Edmonton Oilers

Answers

13. (c) Gretzky scored 50 goals in just 39 games in the 1981-82 season. Only four other NHL players have scored 50 goals in 50 games.

14. (b) The Conn Smythe Award, named for the longtime owner, general manager, and head coach of the Toronto Maple Leafs, is awarded to the MVP of the Stanley Cup Playoffs each year.

15. (b) In the 1970s and early 1980's, the Philadelphia Flyers led the league in penalties and became known as the "Broad Street Bullies" due to their aggressive form of play.

16. How many 20-minute periods are there in an NHL game?

a) 2

b) 3

c) 4

17. What NHL team made it to the playoffs a record 29 consecutive times?

a) Toronto Maple Leafs

b) Montreal Canadiens

c) Boston Bruins

18. Who became the first father and son to win the NHL's Most Valuable Player Award?

a) Bobby and Brett Hull

b) Gordie and Mark Howe

c) Peter and Yan Strastny

Answers

16. (b) There are 3 twenty-minute periods in an NHL hockey game.

17. (c) The Boston Bruins hold the record for making it to the playoffs 29 consecutive times. They accomplished this from 1967-68 through 1995-96.

18. (a) Bobby and Brett Hull became the first father and son in NHL history to both win the league's MVP Award. Bobby won in 1966 and his son, Brett, won in 1991.

19. What NHL player holds the record for most career goals?
a) Gordie Howe
b) Wayne Gretzky
c) Brett Hull

20. Who was the last NHL player to play without a helmet?
a) Craig McTavish
b) Bernie Federko
c) Wayne Cashman

21. What is the most common injury in ice hockey?
a) Knee ligament injury
b) Shoulder separation
c) Sprained ankle

Answers

19. (b) Wayne Gretzky holds the NHL record for most career goals scored with 894.

20. (a) Craig McTavish was the last player in the NHL to play without a helmet. He played his final game for the St. Louis Blues during the 1996-97 season.

21. (b) Shoulder separations are the most common injury to players in ice hockey due to direct contact with other players and the boards.

22. Who was the first NHL player to score 60 goals in one season?
a) Phil Esposito
b) Mario Lemieux
c) Alex Ovechkin

23. What is the official weight of an NHL puck?
a) 3.7 ounces
b) 6 ounces
c) 9.4 ounces

24. Which NHL team almost relocated to Saskatoon after Ralston Purina pet foods sold the franchise in 1983?
a) Buffalo Sabres
b) Chicago Blackhawks
c) St. Louis Blues

Answers

22. (a) Phil Esposito, center for the Boston Bruins, set an NHL record by being the first player to score 60 goals in a single season. He did it in the 1970-71 season with a total of 76 goals.
23. (b) An official NHL game puck weighs 6 ounces.
24. (c) The St. Louis Blues were all set to relocate, but the NHL rejected the move because it didn't want to lose the St. Louis market for one as small as Saskatoon.

25. Which country did the USA men's Olympic ice hockey team defeat to win the Gold Medal in the 1980 Olympics?

a) Canada

b) Finland

c) Russia

26. What NHL superstar is nicknamed "Mr. Hockey"?

a) Jean Beliveau

b) Gordie Howe

c) Maurice Richard

27. Where did the first "organized" ice hockey game take place?

a) Montreal, Canada

b) Anchorage, Alaska

c) Oslo, Norway

Answers

25. (b) Finland. Although most known for defeating Russia in the semifinals, known as the "Miracle on Ice," the USA team then went on two days later to defeat Finland to win the Gold Medal.

26. (b) Gordie Howe. Considered by many to be the greatest all-around player to ever play the game. Loved by fans and respected by players, Howe was a true ambassador of the game.

27. (a) Montreal Canada. On March 3, 1875 the first organized indoor game of ice hockey was played in Montreal's Victoria skating rink between two nine-player teams.

28. What NHL player signed the first million dollar contract in the league's history?

a) Bobby Orr

b) Wayne Gretzky

c) Mark Messier

29. What is the name of the machine that resurfaces the ice on a hockey rink?

a) Zoltairi

b) Zamboni

c) Zenfurhi

30. Who is the Stanley Cup named after?

a) Lord Frederick Arthur Stanley

b) Henry Morton Stanley

c) Earl Watson Stanley

Answers

28. (a) Bobby Orr became the first player in NHL history to be awarded a million-dollar contract in 1971. Reported to be $200,000 per season over five years.

29. (b) Zamboni. The son of Italian immigrants, Frank Zamboni, invented the ice resurfacing machine in Paramount, California in 1949.

30. (a) Lord Frederick Arthur Stanley. Appointed as Governor General of Canada in 1888 by Queen Victoria, Stanley and his family became highly enthusiastic about the game, presenting the Cup for the first time in 1893 to the Montreal Amateur Athletic Association champions, Montreal Hockey Club.

31. In 1967, the NHL undertook one of the greatest expansions in professional sports history when it doubled its roster of teams. Which of the following reflects that change?

a) From 3 teams to 6

b) From 6 teams to 12

c) From 12 teams to 24

32. In what year was the NHL founded?

a) 1891

b) 1917

c) 1934

33. How thick is the ice on an official NHL arena?

a) 1-1.25 inches thick

b) 2-3 inches thick

c) 5 inches thick

Answers

31. (b) In 1967 the NHL doubled in size, expanding from 6 teams to 12 teams.

32. (b) The NHL was founded in 1917 following the demise of its predecessor league, the National Hockey Association (NHA).

33. (a) The ice on an official NHL rink is 1-1.25 inches thick.

34. How many regular season games does each NHL team play each year?

a) 65

b) 82

c) 104

35. Which NHL team has the same colors on its logo as their cities football and baseball teams?

a) Boston Bruins

b) Chicago Blackhawks

c) Pittsburgh Penguins

36. What year did the NHL not play?

a) 1958-59 season

b) 1976-77 season

c) 2004-05 season

Answers

34. (b) 82. Since the 1995-96 season, each team in the NHL plays 82 regular season games, 41 each at home and on the road.

35. (c) The Pittsburgh Penguins have the same colors, black and gold, on their logo as the cities football team, the Steelers, and baseball team, the Pirates.

36. (c) The 2004-05 season. The entire 1.230 game schedule, that was set to begin in October, was officially cancelled on February 16, 2005, due to an unresolved dispute and lockout between owners and players that began on September 16, 2004.

37. What company is the official supplier of pucks to the NHL?
a) Fast Skate Corp.
b) Sherwood Hockey
c) Bauer Company

38. Who did the 1967 NHL expansion team, the California Golden Seals, become in 1976?
a) San Jose Sharks
b) Cleveland Barons
c) Dallas Stars

39. After 26 seasons in the NHL, the Minnesota North Stars became what team in 1993?
a) Tampa Bay Lightning
b) Carolina Hurricanes
c) Dallas Stars

Answers

37. (b) Sherwood Hockey, formerly known as Inglasco, is the official manufacturer and provider of pucks to the NHL.

38. (b) The Cleveland Barons. Never a very successful franchise, the Golden Seals fared no better once they moved to Cleveland in 1976, lasting only two seasons before merging teams with the Minnesota North Stars.

39. (c) Dallas Stars. After years of poor performance and losing support from their fan base, the owners told the NHL they wanted to move to Dallas.

40. Which NHL player holds the record for most consecutive games played in a career?

a) Doug Jarvis

b) Gary Unger

c) Steve Larmer

41. The Norris Trophy is awarded to an NHL player each season for what achievement?

a) Most goals scored in a season

b) The league's best defenseman

c) Most saves by a goaltender in a season

42. Which NHL team was swept in 4 games in three consecutive years in the Stanley Cup Final?

a) Philadelphia Flyers

b) New York Rangers

c) St. Louis Blues

Answers

40. (a) Doug Jarvis holds the record for most consecutive games played with 964, never missing a regular season game in his NHL career (1975-1987).

41. (b) The Norris Trophy is awarded each year to the best defenseman in the NHL by a vote of members of the Professional Hockey Writers' Association.

42. (c) The St. Louis Blues were swept 4-0 in 1968 and 1969 by Montreal and again in 1970 by Boston.

43. What reason are ice hockey pucks frozen before games?

a) To honor an old Canadian tradition
b) To keep them from bouncing wildly
c) To increase their speed on the ice

44. The Pittsburgh Penguins once had a live penguin as their mascot. What was its name?

a) Penguin Pete
b) Hip Check Bobby
c) Hat Trick Harry

45. How many records does NHL superstar Wayne Gretzky hold?

a) 34
b) 61
c) 73

Answers

43. (b) Hockey pucks are frozen before games to keep them from bouncing wildly during play.
44. (a) In 1968, in an effort to bring in more fans after a less-than-stellar inaugural season, they brought in a live penguin as their mascot, who was known as 'Penguin Pete'.
45. (b) Wayne Gretzky holds 61records in the NHL, more than any other player in history.

46. Which NHL player is credited with "inventing" the slapshot?
a) Bernie Geoffrion
b) Bobby Hull
c) Darryl Sittler

47. Which NHL player holds the record for most penalty minutes accumulated in a single season?
a) Gordie Howe
b) Terry O'Reilly
c) Dave Schultz

48. In what year did the longest overtime playoff game happen in NHL history?
a) 1936
b) 1958
c) 1983

Answers

46. (a) Bernie Geoffrion is credited with bringing the slapshot to the NHL in 1951. He was given the nickname, "Boom Boom" because his shot was so hard and fast.

47. (c) Dave "the Hammer" Schultz of the Philadelphia Flyers holds the NHL record for most penalty minutes accumulated in a single season. He had 474 during the 1974-75 season.

48. (a) 1936. The Detroit Red Wings finally beat the Montreal Maroons in the sixth overtime period. They played an equivalent of almost 3 games that night.

49. During an average NHL game, how many hockey pucks are used?

a) 12
b) 24
c) 48

50. In what year was the first official goal scored in the NHL?

a) 1917
b) 1926
c) 1942

Answers

49. a) Twelve pucks on average are used during a single NHL game.
50. (a) The Montreal Wanderer's Dave Ritchie scored the first official NHL goal on December 19, 1917 against the Toronto Arenas.

OK – get out of the penalty box, unlace the skates and head for the SOCCER field!

Here we go!!

 SOCCER

1. What year was the first World Cup held?
a) 1923
b) 1930
c) 1953

2. What is the "correct" name for the area of play in soccer?
a) pitch
b) field
c) arena

3. At what age did Brazilian soccer superstar Pelé begin playing professionally?
a) 16
b) 18
c) 24

Answers

1. (b) The first FIFA World Cup was held in 1930 in Uruguay. 13 teams competed and Uruguay won.
2. (a) The correct name for the area of play in soccer is known as the "pitch".
3. (a) Soccer superstar Pelé started playing professionally at the age of 16. He played his first World Cup at age 17, helping Brazil win its first World Cup in 1958.

4. What does the acronym FIFA stand for?

a) Formation in France Alliance

b) Federation International de Football
   Association

c) Federal Internal Football Agency

5. What country was soccer great, Cristiano Ronaldo born in?

a) Argentina

b) Brazil

c) Columbia

6. Anthony Lopes is the goalkeeper for which World Cup squad?

a) Portugal

b) England

c) Africa

Answers

4. (b) FIFA stands for the Federation International
de Football, and is the international governing
organization of football, futsal, and beach soccer.
5. (b) Soccer star Cristiano Ronaldo was born in
Brazil on February 5, 1985.
6. (a) Anthony Lopes is the goalkeeper for
Portugal.

 SOCCER

7. Who won the FIFA World Cup in 2018?
a) Brazil
b) France
c) Germany

8. Who was the FIFA World Player of the Year in 2000?
a) Zinedine Zidane
b) Oliver Kahn
c) Leo Messi

9. What year was the Major League Soccer league founded?
a) 1971
b) 1993
c) 2003

Answers

7. (b) France won the FIFA World Cup in 2018. They beat Croatia by a score of 4-2.
8. (a) French soccer player Zinedine Zidane was named FIFA Player of the Year in 2000.
9. (b) The Major League Soccer league was founded in 1993. It is a men's pro soccer league and represents the sports highest level of competition in the United States and Canada.

10. In what country did soccer originate as the game we know played today?
a) Brazil
b) United States
c) England

11. What is the circumference of a regulation size professional soccer ball?
a) 35-37 centimeters
b) 68-70 centimeters
c) 93-95 centimeters

12. How many total black and white geometrical panels are on a soccer ball?
a) 26
b) 32
c) 47

Answers

10. (c) England is credited with developing the game of soccer as we know it today during the 1800s.

11. (b) A regulation size professional soccer ball, called a Size 5, has a circumference of between 68 and 70 centimeters.

12. (b) A soccer ball has a total of 32 black and white panels on it. 12 are pentagons and 20 are hexagons.

13. How long can a goalkeeper hold onto the ball for without incurring a penalty according to official FIFA rules?

a) 6 seconds

b) 10 seconds

c) 30 seconds

14. Why did the Indian national team withdraw from the FIFA World Cup competition in 1950?

a) As a political protest.

b) Because they didn't have enough players to field a full squad.

c) Because they weren't allowed to play barefoot.

15. How many players are each team allowed to have on the soccer field during play?

a) 9

b) 11

c) 12

Answers

13. (a) A goalkeeper can hold onto the ball for a maximum of 6 seconds without incurring a penalty.

14. (c) India withdrew from the 1950 World Cup because they weren't allowed to play barefoot per FIFA rules.

15. (b) Each soccer team is allowed a maximum of 11 players on the field during live play.

16. Which soccer team has won the most World Cups?

a) Brazil
b) England
c) United States

17. How many professional level soccer leagues are there in the United States?

a) 2
b) 3
c) 6

18. How often is the World Cup played?

a) Every 2 years
b) Every 3 years
c) Every 4 years

Answers

16. (a) Brazil has won five World Cups. The most of any team in history.
17. (b) There are three professional soccer leagues in the United States.
18. (c) The World Cup is played every 4 years, allowing for qualification tournaments and logistics planning by the hosting country.

 SOCCER

19. What does it mean when a soccer player is given a "red card" during a game?

a) A player has achieved setting a scoring record.

b) A player has been dismissed from the field of play for misconduct.

c) A player has illegally used their hands to control the ball during play.

20. Which country's soccer team helped secure a truce to the nation's civil war in 2006?

a) Ivory Coast

b) Libya

c) Somalia

21. How many minutes of play are in a World Cup soccer game?

a) 60 minutes

b) 90 minutes

c) 120 minutes

Answers

19. (b) A soccer player receives a "red card" when they have been dismissed from the field of play for misconduct.

20. (a) The Ivory Coast team eased tensions between the government and rebel forces by playing a match in the rebel capital of Bouaké, bringing the armies together peacefully for the first time.

21. (b) A World Cup soccer game is 90 minutes in length.

22. Who holds the record for kicking the longest goal in soccer history?

a) Mohd Syamsuri Mustafa

b) Leo Messi

c) Asmir Begovic

23. Soccer legend Pelé played his last game for which team?

a) Santos

b) New York Cosmos

c) Both Santos and the New York Cosmos

24. Who is the only soccer player in history to win six FIFA Ballon d'Or Awards?

a) Christiano Ronaldo

b) Lionel Messi

c) Pelé

Answers

22. (c) Goalkeeper Asmir Begovic holds the record for kicking the longest goal of all time, measured at 100.5 yards on November 2, 2013.

23. (c) On October 1st, 1977, Pelé played his last game as a footballer for both teams. He played the first half of the game for the Cosmos, and the second half for Santos.

24. (b) Soccer star Lionel Messi holds the record for most Ballon d'Or Awards with six.

25. What was the largest margin of victory in an international soccer match?
a) 11
b) 21
c) 31

26. What was the fastest goal scored in World Cup history?
a) 6.2 seconds
b) 10.8 seconds
c) 12.4 seconds

27. Who won the first two FIFA Women's World Player of the Year Award?
a) Michelle Akers
b) Mia Hamm
c) Birgit Prinz

Answers

25. (c) In the 2002 FIFA World Cup qualifying match between Australia and American Samoa, the Aussies won, 31-0.
26. (b) Turkish soccer legend Hakan Sukur scored a goal against South Korea in the 2002 World Cup Bronze medal match just 10.8 seconds after the opening whistle was blown.
27. (b) American superstar Mia Hamm won back to back awards in 2001 and 2002.

28. Which team has played in the FIFA World Cup finals three times but never won?

a) Argentina

b) Holland

c) Germany

29. Which team was the first to win two consecutive World Cups?

a) Norway

b) Russia

c) Italy

30. Who has played in the most games at FIFA World Cup matches?

a) Giuseppe Bergomi

b) Lothar Matthaus

c) Enzo Scifo

Answers

28. (b) The Holland team made it to the finals in 1974, 1978, 1nd 2010 but lost to West Germany, Argentina and Spain respectively.

29. (c) Italy became the first team to win two World Cups back to back when they did it in 1934 and 1938.

30. (b) Lothar Matthaus played in a record 25 World Cup games during his career playing in 5 different World Cups.

31. How much money is awarded to a winning team in a FIFA World Cup championship?

a) $12 million

b) $38 million

c) $55 million

32. Which England player won the Golden Boot Award in 2018?

a) Alan Smith

b) Harry Kane

c) Ashley Williams

33. What team tried to steal a bus at the 1974 World Cup?

a) Chile

b) Russia

c) Zaire

Answers

31. (b) The winning team in a World Cup championship receives $38 million dollars.

32. (b) Harry Kane, captain for the England team won this award in 2018.

33. (c) Zaire. During the 1974 World Cup in Munich, national teams were given BMW buses for local transportation. After being eliminated, the Zaire team unsuccessfully tried to drive theirs back to Africa.

34. What team holds the record for playing in the most FIFA World Cup tournaments?

a) France
b) Brazil
c) Germany

35. What is the record for most goals scored by a player in a single World Cup competition?

a) 5
b) 9
c) 13

36. What country forfeited a World Cup Qualifier after failing to show up for the match?

a) Argentina
b) Morocco
c) Estonia

Answers

34. (b) Brazil holds the record for playing in the most FIFA World Cup tournaments of any team - 21. They have been in every one since it started in 1930.
35. (c) 13. In 1958, Frenchman Just Fontaine scored 13 goals to lead his team to a third -place finish in the World Cup competition in Sweden.
36. (c) Team Estonia forfeited the 1996 World Cup Qualifier match to Scotland when they failed to show up due to a dispute over the stadium's floodlights.

 SOCCER

37. What tradition is practiced by players at the end of most international soccer matches?
a) Trading shoes
b) Kissing on the cheeks
c) Trading jerseys

38. Which soccer player collected the most red cards during his career?
a) Sergio Ramos
b) Gerardo Bedoya
c) Hakan Sukur

39. What is the size of an official FIFA soccer field?
a) 120 yards long by 53 1/3 yards wide
b) 110 -120 yards long by 70-80 yards wide
c) 153 yards long by 63 yards wide

Answers

37. (c) Soccer players often trade jerseys with one another after a match to show sportsmanship and mutual respect.
38. (b) Gerardo Bedoya holds the record for collecting the most 'red cards' during his career, totaling 46.
39. (b) An official FIFA soccer playing field is 110-120 yards long by 70-80 yards wide.

40. What size is the goal on an official FIFA soccer field?

a) 12 feet wide by 6 feet high

b) 24 feet wide by 8 feet high

c) 28 feet wide by 9 feet high

41.The Jules Rimet Trophy was on display in England in 1966 when it was stolen. What was the name of the now-famous dog that found the trophy?

a) Laddie

b) Pickles

c) Shep

42. What soccer team's home field is at Old Trafford?

a) Manchester United

b) Chelsea

c) Liverpool

Answers

40. (b) The size of an official FIFA soccer goal is 24 feet between the vertical side posts and 8 feet high from the ground to the top horizontal post.

41. (b) Pickles, a black and white collie, found the Jules Rimet Trophy in 1966, wrapped in newspaper in some bushes in London.

42. (a) The Manchester United soccer team's home field is at Old Trafford.

43. Which type of football is another term for soccer?
a) European Football
b) Association Football
c) Gridiron Football

44. Who was named Danish Player of the Year four times during his career?
a) Brian Laudrup
b) Christian Poulsen
c) William Kvist

45. Which two countries participated in the first international soccer match?
a) Germany and France
b) Germany and Scotland
c) Scotland and England

Answers

43. (b) The sport of "association football" is commonly called "soccer" in the United States.
44. (a) Brian Laudrup holds this honor and was also named by FIFA as the fifth-best player in the world in 1992.
45. (c) On November 30, 1872, Scotland and England played the first international soccer match in Partick, Scotland. The match finished in a 0-0 draw.

46. Which 2018 World Cup team lost their Nike footwear a week before competition due to sanctions?

a) Russia

b) Iran

c) North Korea

47. Which of the following celebrities owned the Watford F.C. soccer team twice?

a) Elton John

b) Mick Jagger

c) Roger Daltrey

48. Who was the first World Cup Trophy named after?

a) Peter Shilton

b) Jules Rimet

c) Antonio Carbajal

Answers

46. (b) Iran. When the U.S. withdrew from the Iran nuclear deal and imposed economic sanctions against Iran, Nike was forbidden from providing shoes to them, facing criminal penalties and prison if they had done so.

47. (a) Elton John purchased the Watford F.C. team in 1976, sold it in 1987, and bought it again in 1997.

48. (b) Jules Rimet was FIFA's longest running president – 33 years. The trophy is named in his honor.

49. What are the longest sides of a football pitch called?
a) Touch Lines
b) End Lines
c) Pitch Lines

50. In 2006, who took over from Prince Andrew as the President of the English Football Association?
a) Prince William
b) Queen Elizabeth
c) Prince Charles

Answers

49. (a) The longest sides on a football pitch are called the "Touch Lines."
50. (a) At the age of 23, Prince William was appointed President of the English Football Association, replacing his uncle, Prince Andrew, the Duke of York.

Alright! Keep those brain cells fired up! We're moving from the soccer field to the ring – BOXING that is!

Lace up your gloves and prepare for battle!

1. On June 28, 1997, in one of the most bizarre matches in boxing history, which of the following happened?
a) Michael Spinks was disqualified for screaming obscenities at the referee.
b) Fans stormed the ring and started fighting with the boxers.
c) Mike Tyson bit off part of Evander Holyfield's ear.

2. On what date did the last fight of the "bare-knuckled era" between James Corbett and John Sullivan take place?
a) July 8, 1889
b) August 14, 1906
c) June 4, 1924

3. On October 30, 1974, the heavyweight match referred to as, 'The Rumble in the Jungle,' between Muhammad Ali and George Foreman, took place where?
a) Havana, Cuba
b) Kinshasa, Zaire
c) Manaus City, Brazil

Answers

1. (c) Tyson was disqualified from the match and lost his boxing license for this incident.
2. (a) The last "bare-knuckled" professional boxing match was on July 8, 1889.
3. (b) 'The Rumble in the Jungle' was held in Kinshasa, Zaire. Ali defeated Foreman in the eighth round.

4. The term, 'boxing ring' came from which of the following?

a) A painted circle on the floor indicating if a fighter was out of bounds.

b) In the early years, spectators surrounded the two fighters, basically forming a ring around them.

c) From the Olympic Games in Greece.

5. Which following boxer was <u>not</u> one of the 'four kings' of 1980s boxing?

a) Roberto Duran

b) Sugar Ray Leonard

c) Michael Spinks

6. Which boxer holds the record for winning the most world heavyweight title bouts of all-time?

a) Joe Louis

b) Muhammed Ali

c) Sonny Liston

Answers

4. (b) The reason it's called a ring is because in the early days of the sport, spectators crowded around the fighters basically forming a ring.

5.(c) Michael Spinks. The 'four kings' were Roberto Duran, Sugar Ray Leonard, Thomas Hearns, and Marvin Hagler.

6. (a) Joe Louis holds the record for winning the most heavyweight bouts with 27.

7. What was Joe Louis' nickname?
a) The Iron Fist
b) The Brown Bomber
c) The Real Deal

8. What was Muhammad Ali's geographical nickname?
a) Louisville Lip
b) Birmingham Bruiser
c) Philly Puncher

9. How long does each round in a professional boxing match last?
a) 3 minutes
b) 5 minutes
c) 8 minutes

Answers

7. (b) Boxing legend Joe Louis' nickname was, 'The Brown Bomber.'
8. (a) Ali was nicknamed the 'The Louisville Lip' due to his boastful talk before a fight. He was also known as 'The Champ' and 'The Greatest.'
9. (a) Each round in a professional boxing match lasts 3 minutes in duration.

10. Which fight occurred on March 8, 1971?

a) Joe Frazier vs. Muhammad Ali
b) Mike Tyson vs. Evander Holyfield
c) Larry Holmes vs. Michael Spinks

11. Who is known as the father of modern boxing?

a) Randolph Turpin
b) Eddie Gregory
c) James Corbett

12. Since 1987, how many rounds are fought in a professional boxing match?

a) 10 rounds
b) 12 rounds
c) 15 rounds

Answers

10. (a) On March 8, 1971 at Madison Square Garden, Joe Frazier defeated Muhammad Ali by unanimous decision after 15 rounds.

11. (c) Credited with turning the sport of boxing from 'rough and tumble brawls' into a 'sweet science,' American boxer and World Heavyweight Champion James Corbett is referred to as the 'father of modern boxing.'

12. (b) Following the tragic death of boxer Duk Koo Kim in 1982 in a 15 round fight, all boxing organizations moved from a maximum of 15 rounds to 12 rounds in 1987.

13. Which Dutch female boxer portrayed the character Billie Osterman in the 2004 award winning movie, Million Dollar Baby?

a) Lucia Frederica Rijker
b) Claressa Shields
c) Regina Halmich

14. What boxer was stripped of his title, World Heavyweight Champion in 1967, for refusing to be drafted into the US Army.

a) Joe Frazier
b) Muhammad Ali
c) Larry Holmes

15. On February 11, 1990, the underdog Buster Douglas defeated the Heavyweight Champion of the World. Who was Douglas' opponent?

a) Oscar De La Hoya
b) Mike Tyson
c) Evander Holyfield

Answers

13. (a) Lucia Frederica Rijker, professional boxer and actress, starred in this award-winning film.
14. (b) Muhammad Ali was stripped of his title for refusing to be drafted into the US Army citing his Muslim faith and religious beliefs.
15. (b) Undefeated Mike Tyson (37-0) was knocked out by Douglas in the 10th round in one of the biggest upsets in boxing history.

16. In 1947, boxer Jimmy Doyle died shortly after a welterweight world title fight against which boxer?

a) Sugar Ray Robinson

b) Kid Gavilan

c) Sonny Liston

17. Which boxer defeated Larry Holmes preventing him from equaling Rocky Marciano's record of 49 undefeated fights as a heavyweight champion?

a) Michael Spinks

b) George Foreman

c) Muhammad Ali

18. Who was the first boxer to defeat Joe Frazier?

a) Larry Holmes

b) George Foreman

c) Jerry Quarry

Answers

16. (a) Sugar Ray Robinson landed a left hook that sent Doyle to the canvas unconscious. He died several hours later at the hospital.

17. (a) Michael 'jinx' Spinks defeated Holmes on September 21, 1985 in a hotly disputed 15 round unanimous decision ending Holmes hopes to tie Marciano's record.

18. (b) George Foreman ended Frazier's unbeaten streak in Kingston, Jamaica on January 22, 1973, with a 2nd round KO.

19. Who was the first African-American heavyweight champion?
a) Jack Johnson
b) Joe Gans
c) Sugar Ray Robinson

20. What company makes the most popular brand of boxing gloves?
a) Everlast
b) Venum
c) Cleto Reyes

21. In 1974, flamboyant boxing promoter Don King's big breakthrough came when he promoted what famous fight?
a) 'The Fight of the Century'
b) 'The Rumble in the Jungle'
c) 'Thrilla in Manilla'

Answers

19. (a) Jack Johnson became the first African-American to win the world heavyweight crown in 1908, knocking out reigning champ, Tommy Burns.
20. (a) Everlast are the most popular brand of boxing gloves made and synonymous with the sport. They've been around for over 100 years.
21. (b) 'The Rumble in the Jungle' which pitted Ali against Foreman, took place in Zaire, Africa and launched Kings career as a promoter.

22. What was heavyweight champ Muhammad Ali's birth name?

a) Joe Salder

b) Louis Ali

c) Cassius Clay

23. What year was boxing first included in the Olympic Games?

a) 1904

b) 1916

c) 1928

24. In 1952, boxing legend Rocky Marciano won his first world championship when he defeated which opponent?

a) Lee Epperson

b) Harry Bilazarian

c) Jersey Joe Walcott

Answers

22. (c) Cassius Clay was Ali's birth name. He changed it in 1964 after joining the Nation of Islam.

23. (a) Boxing was first included in the Olympic Games in 1904 in St. Louis, Missouri. The United States won the Gold, Silver, and Bronze medals.

24. (c) Marciano defeated Jersey Joe Walcott with a knockout in the 13th round to win his first championship title. During his career he won a record 49 straight fights, 43 by knockout.

 BOXING

25. Who did Roberto Duran defeat in 1972 to win the World Lightweight title?
a) Ken Buchanan
b) Sugar Ray Leonard
c) Carlos Monzon

26. Which boxer became the oldest heavyweight champion in history to win the title at age 45 in 1994?
a) George Foreman
b) Joe Frazier
c) Emile Griffith

27. What is Mike Tyson's boxing nickname?
a) Biter Mike
b) Iron Mike Tyson
c) Mike the Hammer

Answers

25. (a) Ken Buchanan. Duran defeated Buchanan in 13 rounds on June 26, 1972 to win his first world championship.
26. (a) George Foreman holds this record by defeating Michael Moorer in the 10th round in November of 1994.
27. (b) Mike Tyson's boxing nickname is, "Iron" Mike Tyson.

28. Which boxer holds the record for the most career losses by a world champion?

a) Jake LaMotta

b) Sonny Liston

c) Fritzie Zivic

29. How many judges are there in a professional boxing match?

a) One

b) Three

c) Four

30. What is the name of the generally accepted code of rules in the sport of boxing?

a) The Marquess of Queensberry Rules

b) The International Rules of Boxing

c) Broughton's Rules

Answers

28. (c) Fritzie Zivic, from Pittsburgh, Pennsylvania, holds this record, losing 65 fights in his career. He held the World Welterweight Crown in 1940/41.

29. (b) Three judges are seated ringside and are responsible for scoring the fight and assigning points to the boxers for punches landed, knockdowns, and subjective criteria.

30. (a) The Marquess of Queensberry Rules were published in 1867 in London and began being used in the United States in 1889.

31. What professional boxer was portrayed in the 2005 film, "Cinderella Man"?

a) Sonny Banks

b) Henry Cooper

c) Jim Braddock

32. What boxer was the inspiration for Sylvester Stallone's famous movie, "Rocky"?

a) Max Baer

b) Chuck Wepner

c) Tommy Bell

33. Boxer Tommy Hearns had two aliases. One was, "The Hitman". What was the other?

a) The Motor City Cobra

b) El Radar

c) The Manassa Mauler

Answers

31. (c) Jim Braddock. Russell Crowe played the part of boxer Braddock, his boxing struggles, and how he survived the Great Depression.

32. (b) Chuck Wepner. Wepner spent most of his career as a patsy to top contenders, but got his big break in 1975, when he fought (and lost) to Muhammad Ali for the Heavyweight Title.

33. (a) Tommy Hearns was also known as, "The Motor City Cobra."

34. In what year did the World's Fair feature a women's boxing match strictly as entertainment for the predominantly male spectators in attendance?
a) 1904
b) 1933
c) 1962

35. Who was the first boxer in history to become a world champion in eight divisions?
a) Sugar ray Leonard
b) Manny Pacquiao
c) Marvin Hagler

36. Which World Heavyweight Champion got his boxing start while serving time in the Missouri State Penitentiary?
a) Floyd Patterson
b) Bill McMurray
c) Sonny Liston

Answers

34. (a) At the 1904 World's Fair in St. Louis, women's boxing was introduced as entertainment.
35. (b) Manny "Pac-Man" Pacquiao holds this record and was named "Fighter of the Decade" for 2000-2009.
36. (c) Sonny Liston was introduced to boxing while serving time in the Missouri State Penitentiary in the early 1950s and turned pro in 1953.

37. Approximately how many fighters have died as a result of injuries sustained in a boxing match since the Marquess of Queensberry Rules were introduced in 1884?

a) 70

b) 270

c) 500

38. In 1981, Muhammad Ali fought the last fight of his career against whom?

a) Mike Tyson

b) Trevor Berbick

c) Leon Spinks

39. Which heavyweight fighter retired with a career record of 76 wins (68 by knockout) and 5 losses?

a) Rocky Marciano

b) Jack Dempsey

c) George Foreman

Answers

37. (c) Approximately 500 boxers have died resulting from injuries in matches since these modern rules were introduced in 1884.

38. (b) On December 11, 1981, Muhammad Ali fought his last professional fight, losing to Trevor Berbick in the 10th round by unanimous verdict.

39. (c) George Foreman. He was also the oldest world heavyweight champion when he regained the title at age 45.

40. Boxing is also called which of the following?
a) Pugilism
b) Tagging
c) Walloping

41. Which Hall of Fame boxer wanted to back out of an upcoming fight because he had a dream he was going to kill his opponent in the ring?
a) Kid Gavilan
b) Roy Jones Jr.
c) Sugar Ray Robinson

42. In ancient Greek culture, what god is regarded as the inventor and guardian of the sport of boxing?
a) Zeus
b) Hermes
c) Apollo

Answers

40. (a) Pugilism. Coming from ancient Greece, the Romans picked up the sport and introduced the word "pugil" meaning "fist" to refer to a boxer.

41. (c) Sugar Ray Robinson. After being convinced by a priest to move forward with the fight, on June 24, 1947, Robinson knocked out Jimmy Doyle in the 8th round. Jimmy Doyle died the next day.

42. (c) Apollo.

43. Which heavyweight champion has made more money selling grills than from his boxing career?
a) Larry Holmes
b) Joe Frazier
c) George Foreman

44. Who is the youngest boxer to win the heavyweight title at the age 20?
a) Muhammad Ali
b) Joe Louis
c) Mike Tyson

45. What city did the boxing brothers, Leon and Michael Spinks grow up in?
a) St. Louis
b) Philadelphia
c) Detroit

Answers

43. (c) George Foreman reportedly made over $200 million through sales of his "George Foreman Grill", far more than he made during his boxing career.
44. (c) Mike Tyson. On November 22, 1986, Tyson knocked out Trevor Berbick to become the youngest title holder in history.
45. (a) St. Louis.

46. Finish the quote: "Float like a butterfly, sting like a bee..."
a) "Who's gonna win? Ali! Ali!"
b) "His hands can't hit what his eyes can't see."
c) "Who dares to fight the great Ali?"

47. Which trainer was known for being Muhammad Ali's mentor?
a) Dick Sadler
b) Angelo Dundee
c) Constantine D'Amato

48. Which boxer was the first to be pictured on the cover of Time Magazine?
a) Jack Dempsey
b) Muhammad Ali
c) Sugar ray Leonard

Answers

46. (b) "Float like a butterfly, sting like a bee - his hands can't hit what his eyes can't see".
Muhammad Ali's first used this phrase in 1964 in a matchup against Sonny Liston.
47. (b) Angelo Dundee is known for being the mentor and trainer of Muhammad Ali in his greatest fights.
48. (a) Jack Dempsey became the first boxer to be featured on the cover of Time Magazine in September 10, 1923.

49. Which fighter is the only heavyweight to go undefeated during his entire career?

a) Muhammad Ali

b) Joe Louis

c) Rocky Marciano

50. What year did the first televised broadcast of a heavyweight boxing match take place in the United States?

a) 1929

b) 1939

c) 1949

Answers

49. (c) Rocky Marciano holds the record for going undefeated his entire career with a record of 49-0 with 43 knock outs.

50. (b) On July 1, 1939, NBC broadcast the first televised coverage in the United States of a heavyweight fight from Yankee Stadium in New York City between Max Baer and Lou Nova.

Well, did you score a knockout on that round? If not, maybe you'll fare better on the links!

GOLF is up next! Fore!

1. What type of clubs are used for long shots from the tee or fairway?
a) Wedges
b) Irons
c) Woods

2. Which of the following weather conditions will enable a golf ball to travel farther?
a) Dry hot conditions
b) Wet cool conditions
c) It doesn't make any difference

3. In what year was the United States Golf Association founded?
a) 1894
b) 1916
c) 1932

Answers

1. (c) Woods are used for long shots from the tee or fairway.
2. (a) A golf ball will travel farther on a dry, hot day because the air is less dense.
3. (a) The United States Golf Association was founded on December 22, 1894, in New York City.

4. In 2019, which golfer tied Sam Snead's career record of 82 PGA Tour wins?

a) Arnold Palmer
b) Tiger Woods
c) Byron Nelson

5. Which golfer was named the 2004 PGA Tour Player of the Year?

a) Vijay Singh
b) Tiger Woods
c) Jack Nicklaus

6. How many dimples are on a regulation golf ball?

a) 50
b 350
c) It varies between golf ball manufacturers

Answers

4. (b) In 2019, Tiger Woods tied legendary golfer Sam Snead's record of 82 PGA Tour career wins.

5. (a) During the 2004 season, Vijay Singh won nine tournaments, ending Tiger Woods five-year reign at the top of the golf rankings and was named 2004 PGA Player of the Year.

6. (c) The number of dimples on a golf ball varies between types and manufacturers. On average though, a golf ball has between 300 and 500 dimples on it.

7. How many golf balls are on the Moon?
a) One
b) Two
c) Five

8. Which golfer became the first to reach one million dollars in career earnings on the PGA Tour?
a) Ben Hogan
b) Arnold Palmer
c) Bobby Jones

9. What year did Tiger Woods win his first PGA tournament?
a) 1987
b) 1996
c) 2000

Answers

7. (b) There are 2 golf balls on the Moon. In 1971, while on the Apollo 14 mission, Astronaut Alan Shepard placed two golf balls on the moon's surface and swung away.
8. (b) Arnold Palmer. In 1967, Palmer became the first golfer to reach one million dollars in career earnings on the PGA Tour.
9. (b) In 1996, Tiger Woods won his first PGA tournament at the Las Vegas Invitational.

10. What does a "Grand Slam" refer to in the game of golf?

a) Hitting three "hole-in-ones" in a single PGA tournament.

b) Winning all four major PGA championships in a career.

c) Shooting par or under in four consecutive tournaments.

11. What golf course is considered the birthplace of golf?

a) St. Andrews in Scotland.

b) The Royal North Devon in London.

c) Foxburg Country Club in Pennsylvania.

12. Who was the youngest golfer to win the Masters Tournament?

a) Tiger Woods

b) Jordan Spieth

c) Jack Nicklaus

Answers

10. (b) A "Grand Slam" in golf refers to a player that has won all four major PGA tournaments in their career.

11. (a) St. Andrews Golf Course in Scotland is considered the birthplace of the sport and was founded on May 14, 1754.

12. (a) Tiger Woods was 21 years, 3 months, and 14 days of age when he became the youngest golfer in history to win the 1997 Masters Tournament.

GOLF 113

13. What legendary golfer has been struck not once, but twice, by lightning while on the golf course?

a) Ben Hogan
b) Lee Trevino
c) Phil Mickelson

14. Which female pro golfer holds a record of eight LPGA Player of the Year Awards?

a) Kathy Whitworth
b) Nancy Lopez
c) Annika Sorenstam

15. How many holes-in-one has Tiger Woods made in his lifetime?

a) 7
b) 20
c) 64

Answers

13. (b) Pro golfer Lee Trevino has been struck by lightning twice while on the golf course.
14. (c) Annika Sorenstam holds the record for winning eight LPGA Player of the Year Awards.
15. (b) Tiger Woods has hit 20 holes-in-one in his lifetime – the first at the age of six.

16. Which of the following is best when scoring a hole in golf?

a) Par
b) Birdie
c) Bogey

17. How many major PGA Tournaments are there in a season?

a) Three
b) Four
c) Six

18. What are the inside of modern golf balls made of?

a) Mixture of glycerin and water
b) Cork
c) Synthetic rubber

Answers

16. (b) A Birdie is when a golfer scores one stroke under par for a hole.
17. (b) There are four major PGA Tournaments in a season. The US Open, The Open Championship, The USPGA Championship and The Masters.
18. (c) Modern golf balls have centers inside that are made of a special synthetic rubber.

19. What year did the USGA allow steel shafted clubs to be used in play?
a) 1924
b) 1934
c) 1944

20. What city and state is the Masters Tournament played in?
a) Pebble Beach, California
b) Augusta, Georgia
c) Hilton Head, South Carolina

21. Which famous golfer has a refreshing summertime drink of half iced tea-half lemonade named after him?
a) Arnold Palmer
b) Jack Nicklaus
c) Hale Irwin

Answers

19. (a) 1924. Until that time the shafts were made from wood, mostly Hickory. Herbert Lagerblade became the first golfer to use a steel-shafted club in a US Open in 1924.

20. (b) The Masters Tournament is played every year at Augusta National Golf Club in Augusta, Georgia.

21. (a) The popular summertime thirst-quencher, consisting of half iced tea and half lemonade is the 'Arnold Palmer.'

22. How many clubs is a player allowed to carry with them in a PGA tournament?

a) 12

b) 14

c) 16

23. What is a shot called that is three under par on a hole?

a) A Dragon

b) A Double Eagle

c) A Shark

24. Which following golfer is naturally right-handed but golfs left-handed?

a) Gary Player

b) Phil Mickelson

c) Gene Sarazen

Answers

22. (b) 14 is the maximum number of clubs a player can carry with them in a PGA Tournament.
23. (b) A Double Eagle. An extremely rare score, it occurs most commonly on par-five holes.
24. (b) Phil Mickelson. Four-time major champion Mickelson does everything else right-handed, except playing golf.

25. Who was the first non-American to win the masters Tournament?

a) Gary Player

b) Lee Trevino

c) Tianlang Guan

26. What year was the first masters Tournament played?

a) 1929

b) 1934

c) 1961

27. Which golfer invented the modern sand wedge?

a) Sam Snead

b) Arnold Palmer

c) Gene Sarazen

Answers

25. (a) Gary Player was the first non-American golfer to win the Masters Tournament. He was born in Johannesburg, South Africa, and won his first Masters in 1961.

26. (b) The first Masters Tournament was played in 1934. Horton Smith won by two strokes.

27. (c) Golfing legend Gene Sarazen is credited with inventing the sand wedge in 1930.

28. How many PGA Tour wins did Jack Nicklaus achieve in his career?

a) 55

b) 73

c) 96

29. Who was the first winner of the U.S. Women's Open?

a) Louis Suggs

b) Kathy Whitworth

c) Patty Berg

30. Which of the following is the penalty for hitting a ball out of bounds?

a) Loss of one stroke and return to the spot of the previous stroke.

b) Loss of two strokes and play ball where it lands.

c) Return to spot of previous stroke with no loss of strokes.

Answers

28. (b) Jack Nicklaus accumulated 73 PGA Tour wins during his 43-year career.

29. (c) In 1946, Patty Berg won the very first U.S. Women's Open and was a founding member of the LPGA Tour.

30. (a) The penalty of hitting a ball out of bounds is loss of one stroke and return to the spot of the previous stroke.

31. Which famous Hollywood actor is such an avid golfer that he has a clause in his contract that permits him to play golf twice a week whenever he's filming a movie?

a) Clint Eastwood

b) Samuel Jackson

c) George Clooney

32. In the classic golf movie "Caddyshack," actor Bill Murray's character, Carl Spackler, found what in the swimming pool?

a) Judge Smails golf clubs

b) A gopher

c) A Baby Ruth candy bar

33. Which of the following happened at Augusta National Golf Course during World war II?

a) It was used as a getaway for top military brass for rest and relaxation.

b) Cows and turkeys were put on the course to keep the grass from getting out of control.

c) A firing range was built on the course.

Answers

31. (b) Samuel Jackson.

32. (c) A Baby Ruth candy bar.

33. (b) Cows and turkeys roamed the Augusta National Golf Course during World War II in an effort to maintain grass control.

34. In 1457, 1471, and again in 1491, golf was banned in Scotland for what reason?

a) Parliament believed it to be the "devil's work."

b) Parliament believed it interfered with military training.

c) Parliament believed it created "laziness" among the people.

35. What is the diameter and depth of an official golf hole cup?

a) 4.25 inches in diameter and 4 inches deep.

b) 3.5 inches in diameter 3 inches deep

c) 5 inches in diameter and 5 inches deep

36. A "Scratch Golfer" refers to which of the following?

a) A golfer who keeps a poorly written scorecard.

b) A golfer with a handicap of zero.

c) A golfer that heckles other players.

Answers

34. (b) Parliament believed it interfered with military training.

35. (a) 4.25 inches in diameter and 4 inches deep is the size of an official golf hole cup.

36. (b) A scratch golfer refers to a golfer who has a handicap of zero.

37. A dentist designed and was awarded a US patent for an improved wooden golf tee in 1899. Who was he?

a) Walter Hagan
b) George Franklin Grant
c) Bobby Jones

38. Who is the oldest golfer to win the Masters Tournament?

a) Ben Hogan
b) Jack Nicklaus
c) Julius Boros

39. What organization governs the rules for golf tournaments in the United States?

a) The National Golf Federation
b) United States Golf Association
c) The Professional Golf Association

Answers

37. (b) African-American dentist, George Franklin Grant designed a wooden golf tee and received a US patent on it in 1899.

38. (b) Jack Nicklaus was 46 years and 2 months old when he won The Masters in 1986.

39. (b) The USGA – United States Golf Association is responsible for governing the rules on golf in the United States.

40. Where is the World Golf Hall of Fame located?

a) Charleston, South Carolina
b) Poughkeepsie, New Your
c) St. Augustine, Florida

41. In what year did the first televised golf tournament take place?

a) 1947
b) 1953
c) 1961

42. A "mulligan" is which of the following?

a) A tee shot that veers off course and lands in a sand trap.
b) A shot which by mutual agreement between players is cancelled and replayed.
c) A shot that lands on the green from a tee shot.

Answers

40. (c) The World Golf Hall of Fame is located in St. Augustine, Florida.
41. (a) The first televised coverage of a golf tournament took place in 1947 at the St. Louis Country Club in Missouri. It was televised by KSD and the broadcast was limited to the station's local area.
42. (b) A "mulligan" is a poor shot which by mutual agreement is cancelled and replayed.

 GOLF

43. How much money did Jack Nicklaus earn on his first paycheck as a pro golfer at the 1962 Los Angeles Open?

a) $33.33

b) $562.45

c) $1927.86

44. Which golfer has earned the most money in a single PGA Tour season?

a) Tiger Woods

b) Jordon Spieth

c) Vijay Singh

45. Golf balls were originally made from which of the following?

a) Wood filled with lead

b) Leather stuffed with feathers

c) Carved and shaped animal hooves

Answers

43. (a) Jack Nicklaus earned $33.33 on his first paycheck as a professional golfer on the PGA Tour at the Los Angeles Open in 1962.

44. (b) Jordon Spieth holds this record. He earned $12,030,465 during the 2014-15 season.

45. (b) The original golf balls were made of leather filled with feathers, stitched up and then painted.

46. Why are handicaps used in golf?
a) To give the elderly players a fair and equal opportunity to compete.
b) To determine who is the best and the worst golfer in a matchup.
c) To enable players of varying abilities to compete fairly against one another.

47. What year was the LPGA – Ladies Professional Golf Association formed?
a) 1950
b) 1960
c) 1972

48. Where did 'miniature golf" originate?
a) Anchorage, Alaska
b) Pinehurst, North Carolina,
c) Atlantic City, New Jersey

Answers

46. (c) Handicaps are assigned to players to enable a balanced competition between players of varying skill levels.
47. (a) The LPGA was formed in 1950 and is the oldest continuing women's professional sports organization in the United States.
48. (b) The beginnings of miniature, "putt-putt" golf is believed to have started in 1916 in Pinehurst, North Carolina. It soon became a family entertainment craze throughout the United States.

49. What famous golf pro had the nickname, "The Black Knight"?
a) Greg Norman
b) Gary Player
c) Henry Pickard

50. Why are there dimples on a golf ball?
a) The dimples create a tiny layer of air around the ball that cuts down drag, allowing for a smoother flight.
b) The dimples create a 'grip' area for the clubs to contact, enabling consistent shots.
c) The balls look much fancier with the dimples than plain surfaced balls.

Answers

49. (b) Gary Player earned the nickname, "The Black Knight," for his preference of wearing black clothing while on the golf course.
50. (a) The dimples on a golf ball create a tiny layer of air around the ball that cuts down drag, allowing for a smoother flight.

How'd you score? An Eagle or a Double Bogey? Hopefully the former!

Get ready for some love – TENNIS is next!

1. What was the famous matchup between tennis players Billie Jean King and Bobby Riggs called?

a) Match of the Century

b) The Big Racket

c) Battle of the Sexes

2. Who was the first African-American tennis player to win at Wimbledon?

a) Arthur Ashe

b) James Blake

c) Donald Young

3. Which tennis great holds the record for being the only player to have won the US Open on three different surfaces – grass, clay and hard court?

a) Boris Becker

b) Jimmy Connors

c) Roger Federer

Answers

1. (c) On September 20, 1973, Billie Jean King and Bobby Riggs competed in what was billed as the "Battle of the Sexes."

2. (a) In 1975, Arthur Ashe became the first African-American to win at Wimbledon, defeating highly favored Jimmy Connors.

3. (b) Jimmy Connors holds this record. He won on grass at Forest Hills in 1974, clay at Forest Hills in 1976, and hard court in 1978 at Flushing Meadows.

**4. Why did the ITF – International Tennis
Federation introduce yellow colored
tennis balls into the rules of tennis in
1972?**

a) They were more visible to television
viewers than white balls.

b) The board of directors felt they were
"prettier" than white ones.

c) It was cheaper to make yellow balls than
white ones.

**5. Which tennis player holds the record for
winning the most Grand Slam titles?**

a) Andre Agassi

b) Roger Federer

c) John Newcombe

**6. After retiring, which tennis star formed
a band called "The Johnny Smyth
Band"?**

a) Boris Becker

b) John McEnroe

c) Chris Evert

Answers

4. (a) The yellow balls were much more visible to
television viewers than white ones.

5. (b) Roger Federer holds this record with a total of
20 Grand Slam titles.

6. (b) Tennis star and bad boy John McEnroe retired
in 1994 and started the short-lived band, "The
Johnny Smyth Band."

7. What is the name of the Ladies' Singles Champion Trophy at Wimbledon?

a) The Davis Cup

b) The Daphne Akhurst Trophy

c) The Venus Rosewater Dish

8. What type of surface are the matches at Wimbledon played on?

a) Grass

b) Clay

c) Hard Court

9. Gertrude "Gorgeous Gussy" Moran shocked the tennis world when she wore which of the following at Wimbledon in 1949?

a) Lace Panties

b) A Short Skirt

c) A Sleeveless Shirt

Answers

7. (c) The trophy awarded the winner at the Ladies' Singles Championship at Wimbledon is called, "The Venus Rosewater Dish."

8. (a) The Wimbledon matches are played on grass courts.

9. (a) Gertrude Moran shocked the tennis world by wearing lace panties under her skirt at the 1949 Wimbledon, creating a publicity buzz and front-page news worldwide.

10. What company has provided every tennis ball for the Wimbledon Championship since 1902?

a) Penn
b) Slazenger
c) Wilson

11. What year was the first Wimbledon Championship played?

a) 1877
b) 1912
c) 1931

12. What is the name for the left side of the tennis court for each player?

a) Deuce Court
b) Love Court
c) Ad Court

Answers

10. (b) The British company, Slazenger, has been the official ball supplier for Wimbledon since 1902.
11. (a) The first Wimbledon Championship was played in 1877 at The All England Tennis Club in Wimbledon, England.
12. (c) The "Ad Court" is the left side of the court for each tennis player.

13. Which woman tennis player holds the record for winning the most Grand Slam tournaments?
a) Martina Navratilova
b) Serena Williams
c) Venus Williams

14. Which tennis player has won the most 'doubles titles' in history?
a) Roger Federer
b) Serena Williams
c) Martina Navratilova

15. What shape were tennis courts before they were redesigned as we know them today?
a) L – shaped
b) Hourglass shaped
c) Circular shaped

Answers

13. (b) Serena Williams holds the record for winning the most Grand Slam tournaments with 23.
14. (c) Martina Navratilova has won the most doubles titles in history totaling 177.
15. (b) Tennis courts were shaped like an hourglass until 1877 when todays style of rectangular court and rules were introduced.

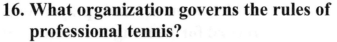

16. What organization governs the rules of professional tennis?
a) The International Tennis Federation
b) The Association of Tennis Professionals
c) The World Tennis Association

17. In a tennis match, a shot that lands outside of the designated playing area is called?
a) Out
b) Error
c) Over

18. Which summer fruit has been served with cream at Wimbledon every year since 1877?
a) Blueberries
b) Strawberries
c) Pineapples

Answers

16. (a) Founded in 1913, the International Tennis Federation is the governing body of world tennis.
17. (a) A shot that lands outside of the designated playing area is called 'out'.
18. (b) Strawberries have been served with cream at Wimbledon since 1877 and are the most popular food item at the matches.

19. A serve that lands in bounds on the opponent's side of the net that goes untouched is called what?

a) Deuce

b) Ace

c) Fault

20. How long was the longest singles match in tennis history?

a) 5 Hours, 23 minutes

b) 8 Hours, 12 minutes

c) 11 Hours, 5 minutes

21. A 'Love Game' means what?

a) A tennis match that has ended.

b) A game that was won without the opponent scoring a single point.

c) A tennis match ending in a tie.

Answers

19. (b) An Ace.

20. (c) 11 Hours and 5 minutes is the record for the longest singles match in history, when on June 24, 2010, John Isner defeated Nicolas Mahut at Wimbledon.

21. (b) A 'Love Game' in tennis means that a game was won without the opponent scoring a single point.

22. Where is the International Tennis Hall of Fame located?

a) London, England
b) Newport, Rhode Island
c) San Francisco, California

23. To win a "Set" in tennis, how many games must a player win?

a) Three
b) Four
c) Six

24. At Wimbledon, the grass on the court must be cut to exactly what height?

a) 4mm
b) 8mm
c) 12mm

Answers

22. (b) The ITF Hall of Fame is located in Newport, Rhode Island and was founded in 1954.
23. (c) A player must win a minimum of six games with a two-game margin to win a 'Set' in tennis.
24. (b) The exact grass height for the tennis court at Wimbledon during tournament play is 8mm.

25. Which male tennis star is the youngest player to ever to win at Wimbledon?
a) Jimmy Connors
b) Boris Becker
c) Bjorn Borg

26. Which official is responsible for ruling the ball in or out of bounds?
a) Line Umpire
b) Chair Umpire
c) Referee

27. Who was the youngest woman ever to win a singles title at Wimbledon in the early era?
a) Margaret DuPont
b) Charlotte Dod
c) Juliette Atkinson

Answers

25. (b) In 1985, Boris Becker became the youngest male tennis player in history to win at Wimbledon. He was 17 years and 228 days old.
26. (a) The Line umpire is responsible for ruling if the ball is in or out of bounds.
27. (b) Charlotte Dod holds the record for being the youngest woman to ever win a singles title at Wimbledon. She accomplished this in 1887 and was 15 years and 285 days old.

28. What material was used for racquet strings in the 1800s that is still used by some professionals today?

a) Cowhide
b) Nylon
c) Sheep Intestine

29. In tennis, the 'Grand Slam' refers to how many major tournaments?

a) Three
b) Four
c) Six

30. What year marked the beginning of the "Open Era" in professional tennis?

a) 1956
b) 1968
c) 1977

28. (c) Dating back to 1875, sheep intestine, or 'gut' strings, were used for tennis racquet strings and are still used and preferred over synthetic strings by many top pros.

29. (b) The tennis 'Grand Slam' refers to four major tournaments – The Australian Open, The French Open, The US Open, and Wimbledon.

30. (b) 1968 marked the beginning of what is termed the 'Open Era' of professional tennis which allowed professional players to compete with amateurs in the Grand Slam tournaments.

31. What year was the first for Wimbledon to award prize money to the winners?

a) 1938

b) 1952

c) 1968

32. What is the most common injury in tennis?

a) Tennis Elbow

b) Sprained Ankle

c) Rotator Cuff Tear

33. What is stationed at Wimbledon to keep the sky clear of pigeons?

a) A hawk

b) A water cannon

c) A siren

Answers

31. (c) 1968 was the first year Wimbledon awarded prize money to the winners. It was also the first year that it allowed professional players to compete.

32. (a) 'Tennis Elbow' is the most common injury in the game of tennis and refers to the inflammation of the tendons that join the forearm muscles to the outside of the elbow.

33. (a) A Harris Hawk named Rufus patrols the sky above Wimbledon to keep pigeons away, which especially like to roost above the centre court.

34. In 1968, sporting goods manufacturer, Wilson, introduced a new tennis racquet made of what material?

a) Wood
b) Stainless Steel
c) Fiberglass

35. In tournament play, who announces the end of the match with, "Game, Set, Match"?

a) Public Address Announcer
b) Chair Umpire
c) Winning Player

36. What are the maximum dimensions allowed per the official rules of tennis for a racquets' hitting surface?

a) 12 inches in length and 8 inches in width
b) 15.5 inches in length and 11.5 inches in width.
c) 17 inches in length and 13 inches in width.

Answers

34. (b) Stainless Steel. Wilson bought the patent rights from inventor Rene Lacoste and marketed the 'T-2000' in 1968 with huge success after tennis great Jimmy Connors adopted it as his own.
35. (b) The Chair Umpire makes this announcement.
36. (b) The maximum dimensions allowed for the hitting surface on a tennis racquet is 15.5 inches in length and 11.5 inches in width.

37. How many bathroom breaks are male tennis players allowed during a best-of-five set match?
a) Two
b) Three
c) Five

38. How many consecutive tennis matches did Chris Evert win on clay courts?
a) 36
b) 61
c) 125

39. How high is a tennis net at the center?
a) 2 feet 6 inches
b) 3 feet
c) 4 feet

Answers

37. (a) Two bathroom breaks are allowed to each player in a men's professional tennis best-of-five match.
38. (c) Chris Evert won 125 consecutive matches on clay courts from August 12, 1973 to may 12, 1979.
39. (b) The official height for a tennis court net is 3 feet high at the center.

40. What is the official size of a tennis court for a singles match?

a) 60 feet long by 20 feet wide

b) 78 feet long by 27 feet wide

c) 80 feet long by 36 feet wide

41. Of the three main types of court surfaces used in tournament play, which one is considered the "fastest" and is favored by "serve and volley" players?

a) Grass

b) Clay

c) Hard Courts

42. Tennis players often "grunt" loudly when serving. Who has the loudest grunt recorded during a professional tennis match?

a) Bjorn Bork

b) Maria Sharapova

c) John McEnroe

Answers

40. (b) The official size of a tennis court for a singles match is 78 feet long by 27 feet wide.

41. (a) Grass courts are considered the fastest type of courts in common use. Fast, low bounces keep volleys short and the serve plays an important role.

42. (b) Maria Sharapova is credited with having the loudest "grunt" when serving, which reached 105 decibels at the 2009 Wimbledon.

43. Tennis was dropped after the 1924 Summer Olympic Games for what reason?

a) A dispute on how to define amateur players.

b) Cheating was discovered by officials.

c) There was little to no interest in the game.

44. What is it called when a player serving misses both serves?

a) Let

b) Foot Error

c) Double Fault

45. The Davis Cup tournament represents what?

a) Amateur players competing against professional players.

b) Professional men players competing against professional women players.

c) Men's teams representing their various countries competing against each other.

Answers

43. (a) Tennis was dropped after the 1924 Summer Olympics Games due to a dispute between the governing bodies on how to define amateur players.

44. (c) When a player is serving and misses both of their serves, it is referred to as a double fault.

45. (c) The Davis Cup represents a men's team tournament between competing countries.

46. Which tennis player became the first British male to win the men's singles title at Wimbledon in 77 years in 2013?

a) Andy Murray

b) Tim Henman

c) Dan Evans

47. Which tennis star set a record for the fastest serve in women's tennis, 129 miles an hour, at the 2007 US Open?

a) Martina Navratilova

b) Venus Williams

c) Anna Kournikova

48. At the 2019 US Open, how much prize money were the winners of the men's and women's singles titles each awarded?

a) $375,000

b) $1.25 million

c) $3.85 million

Answers

46. (a) Andy Murray became the first British tennis player to win the men's singles title at Wimbledon in 77 years in 2013.

47. (b) Venus Williams set a record for the fastest serve at the 2007 US Open at 129 miles per hour.

48. (c) The winners of the men's and women's singles titles at the 2019 US Open each won $3.85 million.

49. The first French Open, played in 1891 is named after whom?

a) Jules Grevy, the President of France.

b) French tennis star Max Decguis

c) French aviator Roland Garros.

50. Which tennis player is the youngest to win the men's singles at the Australian Open and also the oldest to win it?

a) Norman Brookes

b) Ken Rosewall

c) Novak Djokovic

Answers

49. (c) The French Open is named after famous French aviator Roland Garros, who was the first man to fly across the Mediterranean Sea.

50. (b) Australian Ken Rosewall holds the record for being both the youngest and the oldest man to win the Australian Open. He won in 1953 at age 18 years and 2 months and again in 1972 at age 37 years and 8 months.

*Ace or Fault this set? Better lay down
the racket and light your torch,
because next up is the OLYMPICS!*

1. **The 1904 St. Louis Olympics were the only Olympics where distances in the events were measured in which of the following?**
a) Feet
b) Yards
c) Meters

2. **Which African-American Olympic athlete is credited with crushing Adolph Hitler's myth of Aryan supremacy?**
a) Jackie Robinson
b) Muhammad Ali
c) Jesse Owens

3. **Which Olympic athlete holds the record for being the fastest 100 meter sprinter in the world?**
a) Usain Bolt
b) Tyson Gay
c) Yohan Blake

Answers

1. (b) The 1904 Summer Olympic Games in St. Louis, were the only ones in history to measure distances in yards instead of meters.
2. (c) Jesse Owens won four gold medals at the 1934 Summer Olympics in Berlin, much to the displeasure of Adolph Hitler.
3. (a) Jamaican sprinter, Usain Bolt, is the fastest man in history to win the 100 meter with a time of 9.58 seconds set at the 2009 Olympics in Berlin.

4. Approximately how many countries compete in the Olympic Games?

a) 100
b) 200
c) 400

5. Which color is not one of the rings on the Olympic flag?

a) Yellow
b) Orange
c) Black

6. How many athletes in history have won Gold Medals at both the Summer and the Winter Olympic Games?

a) Two
b) Five
c) Thirteen

Answers

4. (b) Approximately 200 countries from around the world compete in the Olympic Games.
5. (b) The color orange is not among the colors on the Olympic flag. The flag consists of these colors; blue, yellow, black, green, and red.
6. (a) Only two athletes have won Gold Medals in both the Summer and Winter Olympic Games – Eddie Eagan and Gillis Grafstrom.

7. Which country is the only one to have won at least one Gold Medal at every one of the Olympic Summer Games?
a) Great Britain
b) Japan
c) United States

8. Which member of the British royal family won an Olympic medal?
a) Catherine Middleton
b) Prince Edward
c) Zara Tindall

9. At which Olympic Games were electronic timing devices used for the first time?
a) The 1912 games in Stockholm
b) The 1936 games in Berlin
c) The 1952 games in Helsinki

Answers

7. (a) Great Britain is the only country to have won at least one Gold Medal at every one of the Olympic Summer Games.

8. (c) Zara Tindall, daughter of Princess Anne, won a Silver Medal at the 2012 Summer Olympics as a member of the Great Britain Equestrian team, riding her horse, High Kingdom.

9. (a) At the 1912 Games in Stockholm, Sweden, electronic timing devices were used for the first time at the Olympic games.

10. Hollywood actor, Johnny Weissmuller, best known for his roles as Tarzan, won five Olympic Gold medals for which sport?

a) Boxing

b) Gymnastics

c) Swimming

11. The Olympic Games were cancelled for the first time due to what?

a) World War I

b) World War II

c) The assassination of US President John F. Kennedy

12. Which Olympian holds the record for being the most decorated, winning a total of 28 medals in both team and individual events?

a) Michael Phelps of the United States

b) Larisa Latynina of the Soviet Union

c) Bruce Jenner of the United States

Answers

10. (c) Johnny Weissmuller won five Olympic Gold medals for swimming events at the 1924 and 1928 games.

11. (a) The Olympic Games have been cancelled three times in history. The first being in 1916 due to World War I.

12. (a) American swimmer, Michael Phelps, holds the all-time record for winning the most Olympic medals, with a total of 28.

13. Which organization serves as the governing body of the Olympics?
a) Official Olympic Rules Organization
b) International Olympic Committee
c) United Olympic Organization

14. Which sport made its Olympic debut during the 1920 Summer Olympic Games?
a) Tennis
b) Baseball
c) Ice Hockey

15. Which Olympic sport is the only one in which men and women compete against each other on equal terms?
a) Pole vaulting
b) Downhill skiing
c) Equestrian

Answers

13. (b) The International Olympic Committee, formed in 1894 in Paris, serves as the governing body of the Olympics.
14. (c) Ice Hockey made its Olympic debut in the 1920 Summer Games and was transferred permanently to the Winter Games in 1924.
15. (c) The Equestrian events, consisting of Dressage, Eventing, and Jumping are the only Olympic sport in which men and women compete together on equal terms.

16. What happened at the 1972 Olympic Games in Munich?

a) The United States boycotted the Games due to conflicts with the Soviet Union.

b) The Ceremonial Doves released at the opening ceremonies were accidentally burned alive at the lighting of the cauldron.

c) A Palestinian terrorist group killed 11 members of the Israeli team.

17. When were the first Olympic Winter Games held?

a) 1924 in Chamonix, France

b) 1932 in Lake Placid, New York

c) 1948 in St. Moritz, Switzerland

18. Which female athlete has won the most medals in Olympic competition history?

a) Skier Marit Bjorgen of Norway

b) Gymnast Larisa Latynina of the Soviet Union.

c) Swimmer Jenny Thompson of the United States.

Answers

16. (c) The Palestinian terrorist group, Black September, held hostage and eventually killed 11 members of the Israeli team at the 1972 games in Munich.

17. (a) The first Olympic Winter games were held in 1924 in Chamonix, France.

18. (b) Soviet gymnast Larisa Latynina holds the record for most medals win by a female with a total of 18.

19. Which team is always the first to enter the stadium at the Olympics Parade of Nations Opening Ceremony?
a) The country hosting the games.
b) The country of Greece.
c) A country is selected at random.

20. What year was tennis reinstated as an Olympic sport?
a) 1964
b) 1988
c) 2000

21. An Olympic Gold Medal is made mostly of what medal?
a) Nickel
b) Silver
c) Gold

Answers

19. (b) The Greek team is the first nation to enter the stadium at every Olympic game in honor of the Games origin to ancient Greece.
20. (b) 1988. Tennis first appeared in the 1896 Games and included through the 1924 Games. It was then dropped and didn't reappear until the 1988 Games in Seoul.
21. (b) Today, an Olympic Gold Medal is made up of approximately 92% silver. The last 'solid gold' medal was awarded in 1912.

22. The Olympics Torch Relay was started by whom and when?

a) The Nazi Party of Germany in 1936.

b) The International Olympic Committee in 1924.

c) President of Greece, Alexandros Zaimis, in 1932.

23. Which following Olympic Games sport made its first and only showing in the 1900 Summer Games in Paris?

a) Tug-of-war

b) Live pigeon shooting

c) Club swinging

24. As of 2021, which country has won the most Gold Medals in the history of Olympic competition?

a) China

b) United States

c) Soviet Union

Answers

22. (a) The Nazi Party developed the Olympic Torch Relay under the direction of Joseph Goebbels and Adolph Hitler. They saw it as a way to illustrate the power and influence of the Third Reich.

23. (b) Live pigeon shooting debuted at the 1900 Summer Games in Paris. It was its first and only appearance at the Olympic Games.

24. (b) The United States holds this record with a total of 1166 Gold Medals won in competition.

25. The Olympic Winter Games sport of "Curling" involves what?

a) Weight Lifting.

b) Sliding stones on a sheet of ice.

c) Rowing a boat.

26. At the 2008 Beijing Olympics, which athlete won eight gold medals, the most to be won by a single person in the Games' history at that time?

a) Shelley-Ann Fraser

b) Michael Phelps

c) Serena Williams

27. Oscar Swahn, a Swedish Olympic athlete, is the oldest person to win an Olympic medal. How old was he when he did this?

a) 54

b) 61

c) 72

Answers

25. (b) The sport of "Curling" involves sliding stones on a sheet of ice and was first included in the Olympics at the 1924 Winter Games.

26. (b) Michael Phelps, the American swimmer, holds this record.

27. (c) Oscar Swahn was 72 years of age when he won a Silver Medal in the 1920 Summer Games for shooting sports.

28. Following the 1979 invasion of Afghanistan by the USSR, how many nations boycotted the 1980 Moscow Olympic Games?

a) 12
b) 27
c) 65

29. Only one person has ever won medals at both the Summer and Winter Olympics in the same year. Who is it?

a) Nadia Comaneci
b) Clara Hughes
c) Christa Luding-Rothenburger

30. The Olympic flag was first flown at what games?

a) The 1904 games in St. Louis, United States
b) The 1920 games in Antwerp, Belgium
c) The 1936 games in Berlin, Germany

Answers

28. (c) 65 nations boycotted the 1980 games in protest to the USSR invasion of Afghanistan, while 80 countries sent athletes to compete.

29. (c) Christa Luding-Rothenburger set this record in 1988, winning gold in speed skating at Calgary and silver in track cycling at Seoul.

30. (b) Created in 1913, the Olympic flag was first flown at the 1920 Summer Games in Antwerp, Belgium.

31. How many countries put in a bid to host the 1932 Olympics?
a) One
b) Five
c) Thirteen

32. Which of the following is the official Olympic motto?
a) Dare to be Great.
b) Faster, Higher, Stronger.
c) Man's Reach Exceeds His Grasp.

33. Why did Bobby Pearce slow down during his rowing race at the 1928 Olympics in Amsterdam?
a) To wave to the crowd of spectators.
b) He dropped his oar.
c) To let a family of ducks pass in front of him.

Answers

31. (a) One. The 1932 Summer Olympics were held in Los Angeles, California. No other cities made a bid to host the Olympics that year.
32. (b) The Olympic motto is "Faster, Higher, Stronger." It was proposed by Pierre de Cubertin upon the creation of the International Olympic Committee in 1894.
33. (c) To let a family of ducks pass in front of him. Pearce still won the race with the fastest time.

34. What do the five rings on the Olympic flag represent?

a) Peace, Unity, Love, Strength, Competition.
b) The five continents of the world.
c) The five original Olympic sports.

35. George Eyser won six Olympic medals in a single day at the 1904 Olympics in St. Louis. What makes this achievement even more amazing?

a) He only had one leg.
b) He was blind in one eye.
c) He had a broken arm during competition.

36. The Olympic games were televised for the first time in the United States by CBS in what year?

a) 1956
b) 1960
c) 1964

Answers

34. (b) The five rings on the Olympic flag represent the five continents of the world.
35. (a) Despite having only one leg due to a train accident as a child, George Eyser won six Olympic medals in a single day in 1904.
36. (b) The first televised coverage of the Olympic Games in the United States took place in 1960 at the Rome games by CBS.

37. Every national Olympic committee has sent women to compete in the Olympic games since which games?

a) The 1960 games in Rome.

b) The 1976 games in Montreal.

c) The 2012 games in London.

38. At which Olympics did the awarding of Gold, Silver, and Bronze medals start?

a) The 1904 Olympics in St. Louis.

b) The 1936 Olympics in Berlin.

c) The 1952 Olympics in Helsinki.

39. At the 1900 Paris Olympics, what was awarded to the winning athletes instead of medals?

a) Jewelry

b) Paintings

c) Motor cars

Answers

37. (c) Since the 2012 Olympics, women have been sent by every national Olympic committee to compete in the games.

38. (a) The 1904 Olympics in St. Louis marked the start of the awarding of all three of the medals; Gold, Silver, and Bronze.

39. (b) At the 1900 Olympics in Paris, paintings were awarded to the winning athletes instead of medals. They were considered more valuable and desirable.

40. At the 1908 Olympics, held in London, a "new" official distance for a marathon race was used that became the standard distance for marathons since. What is that official distance?

a) 25 miles

b) 26.2 miles

c) 27.5 miles

41. Who is the youngest athlete to win a medal in an individual Olympic Games event?

a) Inge Sorensen

b) Bruce Jenner

c) Tom Daley

42. To commemorate which Greek soldier was the Olympic Marathon race named after?

a) Eliud Kipchoge

b) Zeus

c) Pheidippides

Answers

40. (b) 26.2 miles. The change (from 25 miles) was due to Queen Alexandra's request to start the race at Windsor Castle and end at the Royal Box at Olympic Stadium.

41. (a) Inge Sorensen of Sweden holds this record. She was 12 years, 24 days old when she won the Bronze for the 200m Breaststroke in 1936.

42. (c) Pheidippides ran 25 miles from Marathon to Athens with news of the Persian invasion.

43. How much was Paul McCartney paid to perform at the 2012 Olympics opening ceremony in London?

a) $1.57

b) $250,000.00

c) $500,000.00

44. Only one person has both lit the Olympic Flame and also won a gold medal at the same games. Who is she?

a) Rebecca Romero

b) Sheila Taormia

c) Cathy Freeman

45. Which Olympic sport draws the highest number of spectators and television viewers?

a) Synchronized Swimming

b) Weight Lifting

c) Gymnastics

Answers

43. (a) Paul McCartney earned $1.57 (one pound sterling) for his performance at the 2012 Olympics. He had essentially donated his time, but needed to earn some money to make the contracts official.

44. (c) At the 2000 Summer Olympics in Sydney, Australian Cathy Freeman lit the Olympic Flame and went on to win a gold medal in the 400-meter track and field event.

45. (c) Gymnastics consistently draws the highest number of spectators and viewers of any of the Olympic events.

46. Which of the following is involved in the Olympic event of "Dressage"?

a) Skis

b) Horses

c) Paddles

47. Who is the winningest alpine skier in Olympic history?

a) Kjetil Andre Aamodt

b) Johan Clary

c) Marc Girardelli

48. Which Olympic gymnast was awarded the first-ever perfect 10 score on the uneven bars?

a) Shannon Miller

b) Nadia Comaneci

c) Svetlana Khorkina

Answers

46. (b) Horses, often referred to as "Dancing Horses," are featured in the equestrian event called Dressage.

47. (a) Norway skier Kietil Andre Aamodt holds the record for winning the most medals in Olympic alpine skiing with a total of eight. (four gold, two silver, two bronze).

48. (b) Romanian gymnast Nadia Comaneci was the first to receive a perfect score in an Olympic event. She accomplished this at the Montreal 1976 Olympic Games.

49. What is considered to be the most dangerous sport at the Winter Olympics?

a) Bobsledding

b) Freestyle aerial skiing

c) Curling

50. Which of the following is the only Olympian ever to be awarded a Nobel Prize?

a) Golfer Margaret Abbott

b) Gymnast Nadia Comaneci

c) Runner Philip Noel-Baker

Answers

49. (b) According to the International Olympic Committee, the most dangerous sport at the Winter Olympic Games is Freestyle Aerial Skiing, where 49% of the athletes suffer injuries.

50. (c) The only Olympian to be awarded a Nobel Prize was Philip Noel-Baker of Great Britain. He won the silver in the 1500-meter run in 1920, and was awarded the Nobel Prize for Peace in 1959 for his support of multilateral nuclear disarmament.

Ready to knock down some pins? Time to head to the alley!

We're going . . . BOWLING!

1. In 1840, the first indoor bowling alley was built in New York. What was it called?

a) Tubbys

b) Nickerbockers

c) The Kingpin

2. When a person bowls nine strikes in a row, what is it called?

a) Damn Lucky

b) An Octopus

c) A Golden Turkey

3. Which United States President had a bowling alley built in the West Wing of the White House?

a) Thomas Jefferson

b) Harry Truman

c) John F. Kennedy

Answers

1. (b) Nickerbockers was the name of the first indoor bowling alley built in New York.
2. (c) When a bowler rolls nine strikes in arrow, it's referred to as a "Golden Turkey."
3. (b) In 1947, a two-lane bowling alley was built in the White House for President Harry Truman.

4. In what year did the "Professional Bowlers Tour" first air on ABC?

a) 1959
b) 1962
c) 1971

5. What popular television cartoon characters were avid bowlers?

a) Sylvester the Cat & Tweety Bird
b) Fred Flintstone & Barney Rubble
c) Mickey Mouse & Donald Duck

6. Which following person became the first bowler to win PBA titles in six consecutive decades?

a) Don Carter
b) Dick Weber
c) Earl Anthony

Answers

4. (b) ABC television first aired "The Professional Bowlers Tour" on January 27, 1962 in Albany, New York.
5. (b) The hugely popular cartoon characters Fred Flintstone and his sidekick, Barney Rubble, were avid bowlers.
6. (b) Pro bowler Dick Weber set this record when he won a PBA title in 2002.

 BOWLING 165

7. Which bowling pin is called the "Kingpin?"

a) The number one pin-closet to the bowler.
b) The number ten pin-positioned far right in back row.
c) The number five pin-in the middle of the set of pins.

8. What date marks the final episode of ABC Sports, "Professional Bowlers Tour"?

a) September 16, 1983
b) June 20, 1997
c) February 8, 2017

9. What is the official height of a bowling pin?

a) 12 inches
b) 15 inches
c) 18 inches

Answers

7. (c) The "kingpin" is the number five pin – positioned in the very middle of the pin set and often difficult to knock down.

8. (b) On June 20, 1997, ABC aired the final episode of the Professional Bowlers Tour, which was held in Fairview Heights, Illinois.

9. (b) The official height of a bowling pin is 15 inches.

10. Which of the following materials are modern bowling balls made of?
a) Lignum vitae hard wood
b) Rubber compound
c) Reactive resin

11. In what city was the International Bowling Museum & Hall of Fame located until 2008?
a) Albany, New York
b) St. Louis, Missouri
c) Arlington, Texas

12. What is the score when a bowler spares in the first frame and then rolls 11 strikes in arrow?
a) 244
b) 286
c) 290

Answers

10. (c) Since the early 1990s, reactive resin has been the preferred choice of material for bowling balls.
11. (b) The International Bowling Museum & Hall of Fame was located in St. Louis, Missouri until 2008 and reopened in 2010 in Arlington, Texas.
12. (c) The score would be 290.

13. What is the maximum weight allowed for a bowling ball by the Pro Bowlers Association?

a) 12 pounds
b) 16 pounds
c) 20 pounds

14. Who founded the Professional Bowlers Association?

a) Eddie Elias
b) Jay Randolph
c) Pete Weber

15. Which PBA member holds the record for 56 consecutive 200 games bowled in a single tournament?

a) John Denton
b) Norm Duke
c) Jason Belmonte

Answers

13. (b) The maximum weight allowed for a bowling ball by the PBA is 16 pounds.
14. (a) Eddie Elias founded the PBA in 1958.
15. (a) John Denton holds this record. In 1980, Denton bowled 56 consecutive 200 games in a single tournament in Sterling Heights, Michigan.

16. Who became the first women to compete in and win a major men's bowling tournament?
a) Liz Johnson
b) Kim Adler
c) Kelly Kulick

17. Who holds the record for most games bowled in a single PBA season?
a) Dick Weber
b) Walter Ray Williams, Jr.
c) Don Carter

18. It's widely believed that bowling, in its earliest form, dates back to when?
a) Around 3200 BC in Egypt
b) Around 1420 in England
c) Around 1900 in Australia

Answers

16. (c) Kelly Kulick made history when in 2010 she became the first woman to compete in and win a major men's tournament, winning the PBA Tournament of Champions.

17. (b) Walter Ray Williams, Jr. holds the record for most games bowled in a single PBA season with 1300 bowled in 1993.

18. (a) In the 1930s, British anthropologist, Sir Flinders Petrie discovered objects in Egypt dating to 3200 BC indicating early forms of the sport.

19. How are pro bowlers Dick and Pete Weber related?
a) Father and Son
b) Brothers
c) First Cousins

20. Who is the youngest person to ever win a Pro Bowler Association major?
a) Trevor Morgan
b) Anthony Simonsen
c) Marshall Holman

21. What is the official length from the foul line to the center of the headpin on a 10-pin bowling lane?
a) 49.5 feet
b) 60 feet
c) 73.5 feet

Answers

19. (a) Father and son. Dick Weber is the father of Pete Weber.
20. (b) Anthony Simonsen won the 2016 USBC Masters, becoming the youngest person (19 years, 39 days) to ever win a PBA major.
21. (b) The official length of a 10-pin bowling lane is 60 feet from the foul line to the center of the headpin (pin nearest the bowler).

22. Who was the first bowler to roll an official 300 PBA game on television?
a) Pete McCordic
b) Jack Biondolillo
c) Norm Duke

23. What is another term for the "gutter" on a bowling lane?
a) Ditch
b) Trench
c) Moat

24. Which form of bowling was banned in many areas in the United States in the mid 1800s?
a) 9 pin bowling
b) 10 pin bowling
c) Lawn bowling

Answers

22. (b) Jack Biondolillo became the first when he bowled his perfect game in the 1967 Firestone Tournament of Champions in Akron, Ohio, televised by ABC.

23. (c) The "moat" is another term for the gutter on a bowling lane.

24. (a) 9 pin bowling was extremely popular in the United States until around the mid 1800s, when concerns over destruction of work ethic, gambling, and organized crime saw cities and states outlaw it.

BOWLING 171

25. To bowl a perfect game (300), what must happen?
a) Roll 10 consecutive strikes
b) Roll 11 consecutive strikes
c) Roll 12 consecutive strikes

26. Who was the first bowler to achieve over $1,000,000 in career earnings in Pro Bowlers Association Tournaments?
a) Earl Anthony
b) Dick Weber
c) Harry Sullins

27. Which pro bowler holds the record for all-time PBA Tour career titles?
a) Dick Ritger
b) EJ Tackett
c) Walter Ray Williams, Jr.

Answers

25. (c) In order to score a perfect game of 300, a bowler must roll 12 consecutive strikes.
26. (a) Earl Anthony became the first bowler to win over a million dollars in career earnings, surpassing that mark at the 1982 PBA National Championship.
27. (c) Walter Ray Williams, Jr. holds this record with 47 career PBA titles.

28. A "Super Slam" in pro bowling refers to what?
a) Competing in five PBA Title Tournaments
b) Rolling five 300 games in one PBA tournament
c) Winning all 5 major PBA Titles

29. Which bowler was the first to convert the 7-10 split on the Pro Bowlers Tour on television?
a) Parker Bohn III
b) Bryan Goebel
c) Mark Roth

30. Which bowler is tied with Mike Aulby to be one of only two bowlers in PBA history to have won the Super Slam, winning all five major PBA Titles?
a) Dick Weber
b) Jason Belmonte
c) Marshall Holman

Answers

28. (c) A "Super Slam" is when a bowler has won all five of the major PBA Titles.
29. (c) Mark Roth was the first PBA bowler to pick up the 7-10 split on television on January 5, 1980.
30. (b) Jason Belmonte is tied with Mike Aulby, as the only two bowlers to have won the Super Slam.

31. In which of the following countries is the sport of five-pin bowling primarily played?
a) Japan
b) United States
c) Canada

32. What is the minimum degree of tilt that a bowling pin needs in order to fall?
a) 7.5 degrees
b) 13 degrees
c) 18 degrees

33. Which of the following splits are known as a "bedpost"?
a) 4-10 split
b) 7-10 split
c) 5-7-10 split

Answers

31. (c) Five-pin bowling is primarily played in the country of Canada, being invented there in 1908.
32. (a) Due to their rounded bottoms a bowling pin only needs 7.5 degrees of tilt to fall over.
33. (b) A "bedpost" refers to a 7-10 split.

34. What is considered to be the ideal bowling ball speed?

a) 10 miles an hour

b) 17 miles an hour

c) 26 miles an hour

35. For a right-handed bowler, what pins are considered "the pocket"?

a) The one-pin and three-pin

b) The one-pin and five-pin

c) The one-pin and seven-pin

36. A bowling ball comes into contact with how many pins in a "perfect strike"?

a) 2

b) 3

c) 4

Answers

34. (b) 17 miles an hour is widely considered to be the ideal speed for a bowling ball.

35. (a) The key to consistent strikes is to angle the ball into the "pocket." For a right-handed bowler, the pocket is between the one-pin and the three-pin.

36. (c) A bowling ball contacts four pins in what is considered a "perfect strike."

37. When a bowler scores a strike, they receive ten points plus which of the following?

a) The total of the next two balls.
b) The total of the next two frames.
c) Ten bonus points added to their score.

38. Which female bowler holds the record for most PWBA professional titles?

a) Liz Johnson
b) Kim Terrell-Kearney
c) Lisa Wagner

39. Which following company was the first to introduce the fully automatic pinsetter?

a) American Machine & Foundry (AMF)
b) Brunswick-Murray Corporation
c) General Motors

Answers

37. (a) When a bowler scores a strike, they receive ten points plus the total of the next two balls.
38. (c) Lisa Wagner holds the record for most PWBA professional titles, totaling 32.
39. (a) American Machine & Foundry (AMF) was the first company to introduce the fully automatic pinsetter in 1952.

40. In what year did women get their own governing body, the Women's National Bowling Association?
a) 1917
b) 1937
c) 1968

41. Which of the following describes the bowling term "Cheesy Cakes"?
a) Lanes on which strikes are relatively easy.
b) A bowler whose wardrobe is "cheesy".
c) Two consecutive strikes in a single game.

42. What is applied to approximately the front two-thirds of a bowling lane?
a) Carnauba Wax
b) Mineral Oil
c) Furniture Polish

Answers

40. (a) The Women's National Bowling Association, their own governing body, was established in 1917 in St. Louis, Missouri.
41. (a) The term, "Cheesy Cakes" refers to a bowling lane where scoring strikes are relatively easy.
42. (b) Special mineral oil is applied to bowling lanes to protect the wood. The way it's applied can affect the speed and direction of the ball.

**43. Where was the 2011 US Women's Open
Championship held?**
a) Phoenix, Arizona
b) St. Louis, Missouri
c) Dallas, Texas

**44. Which following term describes the act
of bowling without pins, primarily for
technique practice or warm-up?**
a) Ice and Rug
b) Spot Bowling
c) Shadow Bowling

**45. The famous Brunswick A2 pinsetter is
referred to in the industry by what
name?**
a) The Bad Boy
b) The Tank
c) The Apocalypse

Answers

43. (c) The 2011 US Women's Open Championship
was held at the Dallas Cowboys Stadium in Dallas,
Texas.
44. (c) Shadow bowling describes the act of bowling
without pins.
45. (b) Built to pretty much last forever, the
Brunswick A2 pinsetters earned the nickname, "The
Tank."

46. In bowling, a 4-6-7-10 split is often referred to as what?
a) Greek Church
b) Grandma's Teeth
c) Cocked Hat

47. In the movie "Kingpin," which Hollywood actor played the character of Big Ern McCraken?
a) James Gandolfini
b) Bill Murray
c) Jackie Gleason

48. Which company makes the Frantic bowling ball?
a) Bunswick
b) Storm
c) Ebonite

Answers

46. (b) A 4-6-7-10 split is often referred to as "Grandma's Teeth," resembling a mouth with missing teeth. (Sorry Grandma).
47. (b) Actor Bill Murray played the character of Big Ern McCraken in the 1996 movie Kingpin.
48. (b) Storm makes the Frantic bowling ball, a very popular hybrid type ball.

49. Which technological advance in 1967 helped catapult the popularity of bowling for the general public?

a) Automatic Pinsetters
b) Reactive Resin Bowling Balls
c) Automatic Electronic Scorers

50. Who was the first pro bowler to receive a product sponsorship for $1,000,000?

a) Jason Belmonte
b) Don Carter
c) Kelly Kulick

Answers

49. (c) In 1967, Brunswick Corporation invented the automatic electronic scorers for bowling alleys. The ease of playing and keeping score with this technology was a boon for the sport, especially the general public.

50. (b) In 1964, during bowling's popular televised period, Don Carter became the first athlete of any kind to earn $1,000,000 in a single endorsement deal, from bowling ball manufacturer, Ebonite International.

How'd you score on this one?   Strike, Spare, or Gutter Ball (ouch)!

Hold onto the reins!

We're off to the track for some HORSE RACING!

1. What was the first horse to reach a million dollars in wins?

a) Seattle Slew

b) Citation

c) Man o' War

2. What horse was the 100 to 1 shot who scored a shocking victory over Gallant Fox in the 1930 Travers Stakes at Saratoga?

a) Ruffian

b) Kelso

c) Jim Dandy

3. Sir Barton won the Belmont Stakes in 1919, becoming the first horse to do what?

a) Win a major race by 25 lengths.

b) Win the Triple Crown.

c) Win $100,000 dollars.

Answers

1. (b) Citation became the first horse to reach a million dollars in wins in 1951.

2. (c) Jim Dandy, a three-year-old colt, won the 1930 Travers Stakes at odds of 100 to 1, beating Triple Crown winner, Gallant Fox.

3. (b) Sir Barton became the first horse to win the Triple Crown in 1919 at Belmont.

4. Which of the following is the oldest horse race in America?

a) The Belmont Stakes
b) The Kentucky Derby
c) The Preakness Stakes

5. Who was the first female jockey to win a Triple Crown race?

a) Patricia Cooksey
b) Diane Crump
c) Julie Krone

6. What is the longest odds winner in Kentucky Derby history?

a) 36 to 1
b) 50 to 1
c) 91 to 1

Answers

4. (a) The Belmont Stakes is the oldest horse race in America, originating in 1867, it is named after the financier, diplomat, and sportsman August Belmont.
5. (c) Julie Krone became the first female jockey to win a Triple Crown race in 1993, capturing the Belmont Stakes, riding Colonial Affair.
6. (c) Donerail was the upset winner of the 1913 Kentucky Derby. With odds of 91 to 1, this win stands as the biggest longshot victory in the history of the Kentucky Derby.

7. Which following jockey has won more Thoroughbred horse races than anyone in history?

a) Bill Shoemaker

b) Jorge Ricardo

c) Russell Baze

8. Which horse was the first to win the Breeders' Cup and all three Triple Crown races?

a) Seattle Slew

b) American Pharoah

c) Man o' War

9. The racetrack at Churchill Downs is 1 ¼ miles long. How many Furlongs does this equal?

a) 6

b) 10

c) 12

Answers

7. (b) Jockey Jorge Ricardo is the winningest jockey in Thoroughbred horse racing history, with 13,070 career wins as of March 15, 2021.

8. (b) American Pharoah was the first horse to win the Breeders' Cup and the Triple Crown, doing so in 2015.

9. (b) 1 ¼ miles equal 10 furlongs.

10. Where does the Preakness Stakes take place?
a) Long Island, New York
b) Baltimore, Maryland
c) Pasadena, California

11. The founder of the Kentucky Derby was the grandson of which famous explorer?
a) Davy Crockett
b) William Clark
c) John Wesley Powell

12. How many fences do horses have to jump in the Grand National steeplechase race in England?
a) 15
b) 30
c) 38

Answers

10. (b) The Preakness Stakes are held each year at Pimlico Race Course in Baltimore, Maryland.
11. (b) Lewis Clark Jr. – grandson of William Clark, half of the famous exploring duo, Lewis & Clark – decided to found the Kentucky Derby after watching England's Epsom Derby.
12. (b) This race consists of two laps around a track in which horses must jump over 30 different fences.

13. In horse racing, the term, "Going Stick" means what?

a) A jockey running their horse fast and hard on the homestretch.

b) A device used to measure the underfoot conditions at a racetrack.

c) A wager that is placed on a horse favored to win.

14. Which horse holds the speed record in all three Triple Crown races?

a) Secretariat

b) Cigar

c) Tiznow

15. In the history of the Triple Crown, how many horses have won it?

a) 9

b) 13

c) 16

Answers

13. (b) The term "Going Stick" refers to a device that is used to determine the underfoot conditions of a racetrack.

14. (a) Secretariat holds the all-time speed record in all three of the Triple Crown races.

15. (b) Since its beginning in 1919, a total of 13 horses have won the Triple Crown.

16. This horse had an incredible 54 wins in 54 career races. What was her name?
a) Kincsem
b) Goldikova
c) Black Caviar

17. What is the average weight of a racehorse?
a) 800 pounds
b) 1000 pounds
c) 1200 pounds

18. Which horse is not one of the three "Foundation Stallions"?
a) The Byerley Turk
b) The Godolphin Arabian
c) Secretariat

Answers

16. (a) Kincsem was a Thoroughbred race horse who has the most wins of any unbeaten horse in the history of the sport, having won 54 races from 54 starts.
17. (b) The average weight for a race horse is 1000 pounds.
18. (c) Secretariat. The three "Foundation Stallions" – The Byerley Turk, The Godolphin Arabian, and The Darley Arabian are called such because all modern Thoroughbreds can be traced back to them.

19. How many years was it before another horse won a Triple Crown after Affirmed did so in 1978?

a) 13
b) 24
c) 37

20. The winning horse of the Belmont Stakes is traditionally draped in a blanket of what?

a) Roses
b) Carnations
c) Orchids

21. Which famous horse won the inaugural Dubai Cup Thoroughbred horse race in 1996?

a) Cigar
b) Dubai Millennium
c) African Story

Answers

19. (c) In 2015, American Pharaoh won the Triple Crown. This was the first time in 37 years any horse had accomplished this.
20. (b) The winning horse at the Belmont Stakes is draped with a blanket consisting of over 700 carnations, weighing more than 40 pounds.
21. (a) The inaugural Dubai Cup's first winner was future United States hall of fame Thoroughbred race horse, Cigar.

22. What nickname for horse racing reflects the popularity of the sport among British royalty?

a) Royal Racing
b) Steed Chases
c) Sport of Kings

23. What is the name of race horse Seabiscuit's main jockey?

a) Red Pollard
b) Charley Kurtsinger
c) Tommy Luther

24. All Thoroughbred horses born in the Northern Hemisphere in the same year share what in common?

a) Membership in The National Thoroughbred Racing Association.
b) An official birthday of January 1st.
c) Basic training at Pimlico Race Course in Baltimore.

Answers

22. (c) Horse racing has long been referred to as the "Sport of Kings" by royalty and aristocrats.

23. (a) Red Pollard was Seabiscuit's main jockey, riding him 30 times, with 18 wins.

24. (b) All Thoroughbred horses born each year in the Northern Hemisphere are given the same birthdate of January 1st.

25. In horse racing, what is meant by the term, "Break Maiden"?
a) A horse that breaks away from the pack during a race.
b) When a horse wins a race for the first time in its career.
c) To leave the starting gate first in a race.

26. In the 2009 Kentucky Derby, a 50 to 1 odds underdog won with a spectacular performance down the stretch. What horse was it?
a) Musket Man
b) Mine That Bird
c) Mr. Hot Stuff

27. What is the highest price ever paid for a Thoroughbred at an auction?
a) $8.5 million
b) $11 million
c) $16 million

Answers

25. (b) Any horse who has not won a race is known as a 'maiden.' To win that first race is known as "Breaking Maiden."
26. (b) Mine That Bird pulled off a monumental upset, at 50 to 1 odds, by winning the Kentucky Derby in 2009.
27. (c) In 2006, a Thoroughbred named "The Green Monkey," brought $16 million at an auction in Florida.

28. Which horse was the first in the history of the Kentucky Derby to be disqualified after winning the race?
a) Dancer's Image
b) Phar Lap
c) Sea Bird

29. What year was the inaugural Breeders' Cup Classic?
a) 1964
b) 1984
c) 2000

30. The winning horse of which race is draped in fake flowers?
a) Breeders' Cup
b) Belmont Stakes
c) Preakness Stakes

Answers

28. (a) Dancer's Image won the 94th Kentucky Derby in 1968, only to be disqualified three days later after a post-race drug test showed traces of a banned pain suppressant in its urine.

29. (b) The inaugural Breeder's Cup Classic was held in 1984.

30. (c) The Preakness Stakes winning horse is draped with a Black-eyed Susan blanket – except the flowers are fake because Black-eyed Susans don't bloom in Maryland until June.

31. Who was the only horse to beat Man o' War?
a) Affirmed
b) Upset
c) Whirlaway

32. How many jockeys in history have won the Triple Crown more than once?
a) One
b) Two
c) Three

33. What is the average weight of a jockey?
a) 90 to 100 pounds
b) 108 to 118 pounds
c) 120 to 130 pounds

Answers

31. (b) Man O' Wars only loss came at Saratoga in 1919 when he lost in a neck-and-neck finish to a colt fittingly named, Upset.

32. (a) Eddie Arcaro is the only jockey in history to have won the Triple Crown more than one time. He did it twice. In 1941 on Whirlaway and again in 1948 on Citation.

33.(b) The average weight of a horse racing jockey is between 108 and 118 pounds.

34. What is the longest endurance horse race in the world?
a) The Japanese Week Stakes
b) The Melbourne Cup
c) The Mongol Derby

35. What age must a horse be to race in the Kentucky Derby?
a) Two years old
b) Three years old
c) Four years old

36. What set 'Mine That Bird' apart from other racehorses in the Kentucky Derby and Belmont Stakes of 2009?
a) The only bay
b) The only gelding
c) The largest horse in the field

Answers

34. (c) The Mongol Derby is the longest endurance horse race in the world, taking around 10 days and spanning 1000 kilometers.
35. (b) Only 3-year old Thoroughbreds can race in the Kentucky Derby.
36. (b) "Mine That Bird' was the only gelding in the field at the 2009 Kentucky Derby and only the 9th gelding in its history to win this race.

37. What does the term, 'a blanket finish' mean in horse racing?

a) When a jockey uses a whip to get their horse across the finish line.

b) When a horse leads the race from start to finish.

c) A finish so close that a blanket would cover all of the contestants involved.

38. What is an apprentice jockey called?

a) A Bug Boy

b) A Chute Boy

c) A Field Boy

39. Which Triple Crown race is known as the "Test of the Champion"?

a) The Kentucky Derby

b) The Belmont Stakes

c) The Preakness Stakes

Answers

37. (c) The term, 'a blanket finish' refers to a race finish that is so close that a blanket would cover all of the contestants involved.

38. (a) An apprentice jockey is called a "Bug Boy" because the asterisk that follows their name in the program looks like a bug.

39. (b) The Belmont Stakes are traditionally called the, 'Test of the Champion,' because of its 1.5 mile length – the longest of the three Triple Crown races.

40. The three main types of horse racing in the United States are flat racing, harness racing, and _____?

a) Arbitrage

b) Steeplechase

c) Hedging

41. What is meant by the term 'Morning Line' in horse racing?

a) A horse who runs best in the latter part of the race.

b) The fastest time at a particular track.

c) The approximate odds quoted before wagering begins.

42. Where did Citation win the race to become the first equine millionaire?

a) Hollywood Park

b) Churchill Downs

c) Pimlico Race Course

Answers

40. (b) Steeplechase, a horse race which involves jumping fences and ditch obstacles.

41. (c) The term 'Morning Line" refers to the approximate odds that are quoted on a horse race before wagering begins, usually issued the morning before the race.

42. (a) In 1951, Citation became the first race horse in history to win one million dollars in a career at Hollywood Park.

43. What is said about a horse that breaks in front and sets the pace?

a) The horse is a "Shoe In"

b) The horse is "On the Bill Daly"

c) The horse is "On the Daily Double March"

44. In what style of riding does a jockey use a much longer stirrup on the left or inside leg?

a) Acey-Duecy

b) Left-Leggin

c) Off Side Ridin

45. Jockeys stand up in the stirrups during a race in a position known as what?

a) The Blue Hen

b) The Monkey Crouch

c) The Rabbit Squat

Answers

43. (b) A horse that breaks in front and sets the pace in a race is referred to as "On the Bill Daly," and comes from 'Father Bill' Daly, a famous old-time horseman who developed many great jockeys.

44. (a) Acey-Duecy is the term referring to the style of riding where a jockey uses a much longer stirrup on their left leg.

45. (b) The 'Monkey Crouch' is the term used to describe the position jockeys take standing in the stirrups during a race.

46. What year did Secretariat win the Triple Crown?
a) 1969
b) 1973
c) 1981

47. Who owned Man o' War, considered by many to be the greatest race horse in history?
a) Samuel D. Riddle
b) Penny Chenery
c) Diana M. Firestone

48. Who is the most recent horse to have won the Triple Crown?
a) Justify
b) American Pharoah
c) Affirmed

Answers

46. (b) In 1973, Secretariat not only won the Triple Crown, but set speed records in all three races.
47. (a) American businessman and race horse breeder, Samuel D. Riddle owned Man o' War, along with many other famous horses.
48. (a) In 2018, Justify became the 13th horse in history to win the Triple Crown.

49. Throughout Triple Crown history, how many times have any of these three races been cancelled?

a) None

b) One

c) Three

50. The National Museum of Racing and Hall of Fame, founded in 1951 to honor the achievements of American Thoroughbred horses, jockeys, and trainers, is located where?

a) Las Vegas, Nevada

b) Orlando, Florida

c) Saratoga Springs, New York

Answers

49. (a) In the history of the Triple Crown, none of these races have ever been cancelled, making it the longest consecutively running sporting competition in history. There have only been two times in history where slight postponements were made within the year; 1) in 1945, due to World War II, and 2) In 2020, due to the COVID-19 pandemic.

50. (c) The National Museum of Racing and Hall of Fame is located in Saratoga Springs, New York.

Did you beat the odds and bring home a winner on that round?

Last but not least, it's time to switch to a different kind of horsepower –

AUTO RACING!

So, start your engines all you gearheads!

1. Which motor speedway is known as "The Brickyard"?
a) Talladega Super Speedway
b) Indianapolis Motor Speedway
c) Daytona International Speedway

2. What year was NASCAR founded?
a) 1938
b) 1948
c) 1958

3. Which Formula One driver holds the record for most wins in the sport?
a) Michael Schumacher
b) Lewis Hamilton
c) Sergio Perez

Answers

1. (b) Indianapolis Motor Speedway is known as "The Brickyard," getting the name from the surfacing project in 1909 when 3.2 million street paving bricks were laid for the track.
2. (b) NASCAR is the largest sanctioning body of stock car racing in the United States and was founded on February 21, 1948.
3. (b) Lewis Hamilton set a new record of 91 Formula One wins in 2020 at the Bahrain Grand Prix.

4. How many times did racing legend Mario Andretti win the Indianapolis 500?

a) One time

b) Two times

c) Four times

5. Which color strip across the back of a NASCAR racecar signifies a rookie driver?

a) Green

b) Yellow

c) Red

6. Which NASCAR driver was nicknamed "The Man in Black"?

a) Richard Petty

b) Dale Earnhardt

c) Jeff Gordon

Answers

4. (a) Although he competed in the Indianapolis 500 an amazing 29 times in his career, Mario Andretti was only able to win this prestigious race once.

5. (b) A yellow strip across the rear of a NASCAR racecar signifies a rookie driver.

6. (b) Dale Earnhardt earned the nickname "The Man in Black" because of the black Goodwrench livery of his No. 3 Chevrolet Monte Carlo.

7. NHRA drag racers Don Prudhomme and Tom McEwen had one of the greatest rivalries in the sport. What nicknames did they use?
a) The Lion vs. The Tiger
b) The Snake vs. The Mongoose
c) The Grizzly Bear vs. The Wolf

8. This father/son combination won more NASCAR races and season titles than any other father/son combination in NASCAR history. Who are they?
a) Bobby and Davey Allison
b) Lee and Richard Petty
c) Dale Earnhardt Sr. and Dale Jr.

9. Who was the first racing driver to win the Indy 500, the Daytona 500, and a Formula One World Championship?
a) Dan Gurney
b) Parnelli Jones
c) Mario Andretti

Answers

7. (b) Don "The Snake" Prudhomme and Tom "Mongoose" McEwen had one of the most popular rivalries in drag racing, running from the mid-1960s to the early 1970s.
8. (b) Lee and Richard Petty hold these records. Combined they won 254 races and 10 season championships.
9. (c) Racing legend Mario Andretti holds this honor.

10. Which famous journalist raced in the 12 Hours of Sebring?
a) Tom Brokaw
b) Walter Cronkite
c) Peter Jennings

11. What brand car did Richard Petty drive in his first Daytona 500 win?
a) Chevrolet
b) Plymouth
c) Dodge

12. On their ¼ mile run, top fuel dragsters consume how much fuel per second?
a) Approximately 1 gallon
b) Approximately 6 gallons
c) Approximately 15 gallons

Answers

10. (b) Walter Cronkite raced in the 1959 12 Hours of Sebring along with co-driver Peter Baumberger.
11. (b) in 1964, Richard Petty drove a hemi-powered Plymouth to his first Daytona 500 win.
12. (c) A top fuel dragster burns approximately 15 gallons of Nitro Methane fuel on their ¼ mile run (which lasts around 4 seconds).

13. What is the name of the trophy that is awarded to the winner of the Indianapolis 500?
a) The Brickyard Cup
b) The Borg-Warner Trophy
c) The "Wally"

14. Which driver won the inaugural Daytona 500 in 1959?
a) Lee Beauchamp
b) Speedy Johnson
c) Lee Petty

15. Who was the first woman to win in drag racing's NHRA Top Fuel?
a) Shirley Muldowney
b) Cortney Force
c) Barbara Hamilton

Answers

13. (b) The winner of the Indianapolis 500 is awarded The Borg-Warner Trophy, commissioned in 1935 and valued at more than $1 million.
14. (c) Lee Petty. While Beauchamp was able to celebrate the win immediately after the race, Petty was declared the winner 61 hours later after officials reviewed photos and newsreel footage.
15. (a) In 1976, drag racing legend Shirley Muldowney became the first woman to win in NHRA Top Fuel competition.

16. Since 2012, Formula One has held an annual racing event in what city in the United States?

a) Long Beach, California

b) Austin, Texas

c) Miami, Florida

17. Wally Parks, a famous figure in drag racing, is best known for what?

a) He broke the 300 mph barrier.

b) He founded the NHRA.

c) He pioneered the rear engine dragster.

18. The Indianapolis Motor Speedway spans how many acres?

a) 69

b) 111

c) 253

Answers

16. (b) Since 2012, Austin, Texas is the only city in the United States that has held an annual Formula One Championship racing event – The United States Grand Prix.

17. (b) Drag racing legend, Wally Parks founded the NHRA – The National Hot Rod Association in 1951 to create a governing body and help promote drag racing in the United States.

18. (c) The complex that is the Indianapolis Motor Speedway spans a whopping 253 acres.

19. Which American-made car company became the first to win the 24 Hours of Le Mans in 1966?
a) Chevrolet
b) Ford
c) Chrysler

20. Approximately how many hours does it take to complete the Baja 1000 off road race?
a) 8-13
b) 20-25
c) 32-37

21. Which Hollywood actor did all of his own driving scenes without the use of a double in the 1966 film, "Grand Prix"?
a) Steve McQueen
b) Paul Newman
c) James Garner

Answers

19. (b) Ford Motor Company became the first American car company to win at Le Mans, posting first, second and third place in Ford's GT40 race cars.
20. (b) Widely considered to be the most demanding endurance race in the world, the Baja 1000 typically takes 20-25 hours to complete.
21. (c) Actor James Garner, an accomplished driver, handled all of his driving scenes himself in this classic auto racing movie.

22. In 1969, NASCAR banned which car from racing due to its dominance, speed, and performance.

a) Ford Mustang Mach I

b) Dodge Charger Daytona

c) Chevrolet Monte Carlo

23. Racing legend Don "Big Daddy" Garlits is known for racing what type of cars?

a) NASCAR stock cars

b) Indy cars

c) Top Fuel dragsters

24. Which driver holds the record for most career wins at the prestigious 24 Hours of Le Mans?

a) Michael Schumacher

b) Tom Kristensen

c) Jacky Ickx

Answers

22. (b) The Dodge Charger Daytona so dominated the field, that in 1969 NASCAR banned it from racing, determining it would have an unfair advantage over the competition on the NASCAR tracks.

23. (c) Known as the "King of the Dragsters," Don Garlits won an impressive 144 national events racing Top Fuel dragsters.

24. (b) Tom Kristensen is known as "Mr. Le Mans" in motorsport circles, winning this race an incredible 9 times.

25. In 1975, Dale Earnhardt drove in his first Winston Cup race at Charlotte Motor Speedway. What brand of car did he drive?
a) Chevrolet
b) Pontiac
c) Dodge

26. What does the term "banking" refer to in NASCAR?
a) The angle at which a tire makes contact with the track surface.
b) The sloping of the racetrack.
c) The drivers who earn the big money at a race.

27. "Funny Cars" are sanctioned by what racing organization?
a) NASCAR
b) IMSA
c) NHRA

Answers

25. (c) In his debut NASCAR Winston Cup appearance in 1975, racing legend Dale Earnhardt drove a 1975 Dodge.
26. (b) In NASCAR racing, the term "banking" refers to the sloping angle of the racetrack.
27. (c) Top Fuel "Funny Cars" are basically dragsters with bodies and are officially sanctioned by the National Hot Rod Association – NHRA.

28. In what year was the first NASCAR race nationally televised from the races start to its finish?

a) 1968

b) 1979

c) 1986

29. Which driver set a record for the fastest quarter mile in a dragster in 2005?

a) Tony Schumacher

b) Kenny Bernstein

c) Larry Dixon

30. The World of Outlaws feature what kind of race cars?

a) Indy style cars

b) Sprint cars

c) Off-road cars

Answers

28. (b) 1979 was the first year that a NASCAR race was nationally televised from start to finish – it was the Daytona 500 and was won by Richard Petty.

29. (a) Tony Schumacher set a Top Fuel record in 2005 for the quarter mile in 3.667 seconds at 337.58 mph.

30. (b) The World of Outlaws feature Sprint cars that have large adjustable wings on their top and large rear tires.

31. "Big Daddy" Don Garlits is credited with what safety innovation in drag racing?

a) Installing a parachute on the car to slow down.

b) The use of a fireproof suit for the driver.

c) Putting the engine behind the driver.

32. Stock car racing in the United States has its origins in what?

a) The Pony Express

b) Bootlegging during Prohibition

c) The Olympics

33. Which driver won the inaugural Indianapolis 500 in 1911?

a) Joe Dawson

b) Howdy Wilcox

c) Ray Harroun

Answers

31. (c) Racing legend "Big Daddy" Don Garlits is credited with the safety innovation of mounting the engine behind the driver on dragsters instead of the traditional placement in front of them.

32. (b) Stock car racings origins lie in the drivers who ran bootleg whiskey in the Appalachian region of America, using fast cars and driving skills to evade police on the backroads.

33. (c) Ray Harroun won the first Indianapolis 500 race in 1911 with an average speed of 74 miles an hour.

34. At what race does the winning driver drink milk in a victory celebration?

a) Daytona 500

b) United States Grand Prix

c) Indianapolis 500

35.Which brand of tires are used at NASCAR national series races?

a) Goodyear

b) Firestone

c) Bridgestone

36. How many drivers have won the Indianapolis 500 a record 4 times?

a) 2

b) 3

c) 4

Answers

34. (c) The tradition of the winner of the Indianapolis 500 drinking a pint of milk at the end of the race was started by winner Louis Meyer in 1936.

35. (a) Goodyear is the official tire sponsor of NASCAR and is the longest continuous running partner with NASCAR – since 1954.

36. (c) Only 4 drivers have ever won the Indianapolis 500 4 times – A.J. Foyt, Al Unser, Rick Mears, and most recently, Helio Castroneves.

37. NASCAR legend Richard Petty's sponsor for many years was STP. What does STP stand for?
a) Scientifically Treated Petroleum
b) Standard Temperature & Pressure
c) Slick, Thick & Pure

38. Which make and model car has been the official pace car at the Indianapolis 500 the most times?
a) Ford Mustang
b) Chevrolet Corvette
c) Chevrolet Camaro

39. In what year did NASCAR legend Dale Earnhardt tragically die in a crash at the Daytona 500?
a) 1999
b) 2001
c) 2003

Answers

37. (a) "STP" first sponsored racing legend Richard Petty in 1972. STP is an engine oil additive and stands for, "Scientifically Treated Petroleum."
38. (b) The Chevrolet Corvette holds the record for most appearances as a pace car in the Indianapolis 500 with 18 appearances as of 2021.
39. (b) In a tragic last lap crash, Dale Earnhardt lost his life at the 2001 Daytona 500.

40. How many convertibles raced in the first Daytona 500?

a) 0

b) 7

c) 20

41. Who was the first woman to compete in the Indianapolis 500 and the Daytona 500?

a) Shirley Muldowney

b) Janet Guthrie

c) Danica Patrick

42. What strange event happened at the 1950 inaugural running of the 12 Hours of Sebring race?

a) The Florida Governor was given a tour of the racetrack during the actual race.

b) A small aircraft landed on the track thinking it was an airfield.

c) There was a 21-car pile-up on the first lap of the race.

Answers

40. (c) 20 of the 59 cars in the 1959 Daytona 500 were convertibles.

41. (b) Janet Guthrie was the first woman to qualify for and compete in the Indianapolis 500 and the Daytona 500 – both in the same year – 1977.

42. (a) Florida Governor Fuller Warren was driven for a lap around the track by promoter Alec Ulmann while the race was in progress.

43. What famous car maker rivalry played out in the mid-1960s?
a) Ford verses Ferrari
b) Peugeot verses Chrysler
c) General Motors verses Jaguar

44. Who is the winningest Funny Car driver in NHRA drag racing history?
a) Don Prudhomme
b) John Force
c) Ron Capps

45. What 1990 movie about NASCAR racing featured actor Tom Cruise?
a) Talladega Nights
b) Days of Thunder
c) Speedway

Answers

43. (a) Henry Ford II and Enzo Ferrari battled each other fiercely for racing dominance in the 1960s, specifically Ford's desire to beat Ferrari at Le Mans – which they did in 1966.

44. (b) John Force holds the record with an astounding 153 wins and 16 championships in NHRA Funny Car racing.

45. (b) Capitalizing on the growing popularity of NASCAR in 1990, Hollywood made the movie, "Days of Thunder," featuring actor Tom Cruise, portraying real-life driver Tim Richmond.

46. What is a HANS device?
a) A supercharger pulley
b) A special lug-nut tool
c) A safety device

47. NASCAR legend Richard Petty left the sport of stock car racing for a brief time in 1965, switching over to what sport?
a) Drag racing
b) Off-road racing
c) Formula One racing

48. How many members are there in a NASCAR pit crew?
a) 5
b) 7
c) 9

Answers

46. (c) A 'HANS' – Head and Neck Support -is a safety device designed by Dr. Robert Hubbard in 1986 to help keep a driver's head and neck in place during an impact. Widely used and mandated in many auto racing sanctioning bodies today.
47. (a) Petty left NASCAR in protest when they banned the Chrysler Hemi engine in 1965, switching over to drag racing. When the Hemi was reinstated later that season, Petty returned to NASCAR.
48. (b) There are 7 members on a NASCAR pit crew.

49. Which car manufacturer holds the record for most wins at the 24 Hours of Le Mans?

a) Porsche

b) Ferrari

c) Audi

50. Which famous Formula One driver is known as the "Flying Scot?"

a) David Coulthard

b) Jim Clark

c) Jackie Stewart

Answers

49. (a) Porsche is the winningest car manufacturer to compete in the 24 Hours of Le Mans with a total of 19 victories.

50. (c) Racing legend Sir John Young "Jackie" Stewart is known as the "Flying Scot," winning 27 races and 3 World Championship Titles in his career.

Well, there you have it! You've made it to the end and are probably one of the smartest people you know!

"Amazing Sports Trivia"!
12 Incredible Sports with 600 fascinating questions and answers. I hope it's been a lot of fun and laughs for you, your family, and friends as you played along!

Thank you for your support in buying this book! It was a fascinating and rewarding experience for me as I researched and wrote it!

Wishing you all the best that life has to offer!

Michael

ABOUT THE AUTHOR

Michael Schlueter is an author and photographer living with his wife Jill on a small farm in Missouri along with a variety of pets and critters. He enjoys spending time in the great outdoors, seeing new places, and sharing laughs with family and friends.

Other books by Michael include;

"101 Quirky & Crazy Phrases & Sayings"
"Another 101 Quirky & Crazy Phrases & Sayings"
"The Third 101 Quirky & Crazy Phrases & Sayings"
"That's the Fact Jack-101 Strange but True Facts"
"Keep Your Eye on the Ball-Classic Sports Phrases"

and the coffee-table fine art photography book;
"America's Bloodiest 47 Acres-Inside the Missouri State Penitentiary"

Visit Michael and see more of his work at;

www.schlueterphoto.com
www.amazon.com/author/michaelschlueter

I hope you've enjoyed this book! If so, please take a moment to leave a review on Amazon for me. Your support is very much appreciated! Thank you!

All the Best,
Michael